Waking Up in the South

Manifest Your Life. Rewire Your Old Beliefs.

Crystal Brooke Coleman

Copyright © 2025 by Crystal Brooke Coleman
First Edition
Published July 31, 2025 by Marketing Company, LLC, The
Edited by Sarah Grady

This book can serve as an essence for all religions and spiritual practices. It is not written from one particular theory or doctrine but from my own personal experiences and study. It is the love that resides within me that seeks to share information that connects us, not divides us.

If at any time something I share feels in conflict with your core or religious beliefs, I invite you to process it from a place of coherence rather than separation. Nothing I believe or express is intended to persuade or alter anyone's beliefs to reflect my own, but rather to help you tap into the internal compass you already possess. Everything I offer here can be adopted as an enhancement not a contradiction to your faith.

This book was purposefully created by Crystal Brooke Coleman to empower and connect us all.

No portion of this book may be reproduced in any form without written permission from the publisher or author, except as permitted by U.S. copyright law. Please use this book for your own personal development only.

Books may be purchased for educational, business, or promotional use. For sales and bulk pricing information, contact:
email@themarketingcompanywebsite.com

Contents

Acknowledgements	1
Introduction	7
Author's Note	9
How To Use This Book	15
Module 1	19
1.1 Understanding the Law of Attraction	
1.2 Exploring the Power of Manifestation	
1.3 Unraveling the Connection Between Thoughts and Reality	
Our Surroundings Impact Our Growth	53
Subconscious Reflection	56
Personal Story	59
Journal Entry	67
Module 2	70
2.1 Meditation for Manifestation	
2.2 Mindfulness Practices to Enhance Focus	

2.3 Visualization Mastery

Be Here Now	105
Personal Story	108
Journal Entry	117
Module 3	119

    3.1 Building a Strong Manifestation Foundation

    3.2 Identifying and Overcoming Limiting Beliefs

The Ego Trap	135
Personal Story	138
Journal Entry	145
MODULE 4	148

    4.1 Defining Personal Purpose and Intentional Goals

    4.2 Practical Steps to Manifestation

Personal Story	156
Master Your Emotions	163
Illuminate Your Mind	165
Personal Story	169
Journal Entry	172

MODULE 5 — 175
    5.1 Creating Personalized Affirmations
    5.2 Setting Powerful Intentions

Break Free From The Mind Trap — 182

Personal Story — 186

Journal Entry — 190

MODULE 6 — 193
    6.1 Becoming a Conscious Creator
    6.2 Trusting the Process: Embracing the Unknown
    6.3 The Infinite Journey: Manifesting as a Lifelong Practice

Personal Story — 201

Journal Entry — 208

MODULE 7 — 211

Personal Story — 220

Resources as You Continue Your Journey — 226

Manifestation Is an Initiation — 228

The Stories We Carry: The Initiation of Truth — 230

Pain Into Power: A Final Prayer — 235

Glossary — 243

Acknowledgements

To my daughters, Emalyn and River, you are my WHY. Because of you, I keep growing- I keep learning. Not just how to be a better mom, but how to be a better human. Raising you is the greatest joy and the most humbling privilege of my life.

May you see the world with open eyes and eager hearts. May you manifest the lives you desire, and never doubt that you are worthy of everything good this world has to offer.

To my wonderful marketing assistant and dear friend, CJ, miles apart, but close to my heart, your genuine soul and creative spirit have made all the difference in bringing this book to life. Thank you for not only your hard work and dedication but also for just being you- a calming, reassuring presence in my life.

To all the mentors who have illuminated my path with wisdom and guidance, and to every soul who has uplifted me or believed in me, even when I struggled to believe in myself: your presence in my life has been a beacon of hope and inspiration that led me to find myself and my purpose. I am forever grateful.

I would like to extend a heartfelt acknowledgement to Eckhart Tolle and the life-changing impact of his book, *The Power of Now*. This single book, given I read it at the time in my life I was ready to receive it, was the gateway to my spiritual journey.

Infinite gratitude to God and the Universe for the gift of waking up each day, embracing the journey laid before me with renewed purpose and possibility.

Last but not least, to the beautiful soul who entered my life not just as an editor but as a midwife of words, thank you Sarah.

How fitting that your life's work includes helping women birth life into the world, because you have done the very same for this book. Your hands, which have held newborns and comforted mothers, have also held my pages with care, compassion, and a fierce dedication to seeing them come to life.

ACKNOWLEDGEMENTS

With your conversations came clarity. With your suggestions came strength. With your edits came peace.

I am forever grateful, not just for your skill, but for your heart, your timing, your encouragement, and your friendship.

-XoXo

INTRODUCTION

In 2025, manifestation is everywhere. Vision boards, affirmations, and influencers promise instant results. But let's be real. Most of it feels like a shortcut, quick fix, or Easy-Bake Oven spirituality that looks good on the outside but leaves you hungry for something real.

This book isn't about manifesting from the surface. It's about going inward to the places most people avoid. Because real manifestation isn't magic. It's a mindset. A lifestyle. A daily decision to face your patterns, shift your energy, and take aligned action. Manifestation is not external. It doesn't happen "out there". It is internal, it happens within. And no you don't have to be a guru on a mountain top to practice it. Trust me, I'm a Southern girl from Georgia who was simply *ready* to change her life. So I did.

I won't sugarcoat it. The work is real. But if you're reading this introduction, something tells me *you're* ready.

You're done chasing peace. You want to *feel* it.

You're done with fake-it-'til-you-make-it healing. You want something authentic.

You're ready to remember who you are and create a life that finally feels like home.

Welcome, sister. This is the exact moment you were meant to find this book. I can't wait to see where the journey takes you!

Author's Note

"I 'played pretty' on stage, and I played it well. I learned that being fake wasn't just accepted, it was rewarded."

I didn't set out to write a book about waking up. I just kept waking up, again and again, until I couldn't unsee what I had seen. The more I questioned my beliefs, the more I realized how many of them weren't mine at all. They were inherited. Woven into my mind from church pews, school systems, and the DNA of deep Southern pride.

I was raised in the South, where appearances mattered more than truth. Charm was currency, but behind the smiles were contradictions I couldn't ignore, even as a child. I learned to play the part. By the time I was five, I had won over a hundred pageant trophies. I had mastered the toe point, the perfect smile, eye contact, and flawless poise.

I "played pretty" on stage, and I played it well. I learned that being fake wasn't just accepted, it was rewarded. I had the crowns and trophies to prove it. So, I became what the world clapped for. Pretty on the outside.

But underneath the sparkle, I was starting to disappear from myself.

As an adult, I saw the same performance all around me, just in different clothes. I watched men with big egos mask their unresolved childhood wounds with power, money, and the need to control. I had been playing pretty my entire life, and now I was doing it in the boardroom, acting submissive, being likable, polished, and cute for these men.

I was tired. Tired of pretending everything was okay. Tired of calling dysfunction normal. Tired of shrinking to fit into a life that never really fit me. Tired of my appearance holding more weight than authenticity.

This book was born out of that unraveling. It's part memoir, part manual. It holds the tools I used to wake up. Practical strategies rooted in mindset, energy, neuroscience, and aligned action. More than that, it holds truth. Mine, and hopefully yours, too.

You'll read about the cracks in my foundation. Like, discovering that the preacher who married me is now serving a life sentence for multiple counts of child molestation. Around here, appearances are often enough to win over small minds and seeking hearts. If someone looks the part, they are rarely questioned.

That contradiction didn't break me, but it confirmed the quiet disconnect I had carried for years. Over time, I realized many of the people I was taught to follow-the preachers, politicians, or loudest voices in the room-were often the most wounded or the most dangerous.

These truths didn't hit all at once. They came in waves. Private reckonings that stripped away the mask I had learned to apply so well.

This is not a book about being better than where we came from. It's about becoming more of who we really are. It's about learning to rise, not above others, but from within. When we lead with love and alignment, others feel it. They soften. That's how we grow together.

As I mentioned in the introduction, I am no guru sitting cross legged on a mountain top. I'm a Southern woman who once rolled her eyes at the word manifestation. Ten years ago, I would've thought this was nonsense. Now, I'm living proof that alchemy is real. That faith, psychology, science, and surrender all work together. That freedom lives on the other side of fear.

This started as a workbook for MANIFESTED, one of the international retreats I lead. But the message kept growing. The truth kept deepening. Eventually, I realized this wasn't just a workbook. *It was my life.* I'm honored to share it with you through this book.

If I can rewire my beliefs, so can you.

The format of this book is simple. Bite-sized modules you can move through at your own pace. Each chapter is a doorway, not a rulebook. You'll learn how to spot limiting beliefs, shift your energy, and co-create a life that aligns with YOUR truth.

You'll also find stories. Stories of breakdown and breakthrough. Of science and spirit. Of religion and rebellion. I speak plainly, not perfectly. But most importantly, I speak as myself.

This book is not a map. It's a mirror. It's a compass. It's a call to remember.

Before we begin, here is my prayer for you:

May you find strength to tune out the noise of the world. May you feel safe enough to turn inward, instead. May you trust yourself enough to listen. May you honor what you hear. May this book offer clarity where there's been confusion, and faith where there's been fear. May it help you remember: the power was never outside of you. The power always was *you*. May you believe.

Much love,

Brooke, aka Pretty

How To Use This Book

As I mentioned in the Author's Note, this book was originally conceived as a manual for my yoga retreats called, MANIFESTED. As such, the order of the modules presented in this book adhere to my retreat schedule. My suggestion is to read the modules in order, all the way through, so you can get a general idea of the concepts presented. Then, as you return to the book throughout your manifestation journey, feel free to reference the modules in any order you feel inspired to.

Repetition is Key

You'll notice that several modules repeat key concepts introduced in previous modules; this is intentional. That way, if you don't always want to read the book in order, you are still getting the core teachings necessary to properly propel your manifestation journey. Plus, repetition is the key to absorbing and applying new skills more effectively and confidently!

Practical and Personal

In addition to core manifestation teachings, you'll notice that this book also provides memoir-style personal stories and reflections connected to each module's theme. Additionally, you'll notice journal prompts and exercises at the end of each module to further support your integration process.

This book is both practical *and* personal. *Waking Up in The South* isn't about perfecting the skills of manifestation. It's about introducing these skills, and then sharing the beautiful, and often messy, journey of ***becoming*** that naturally unfolds when we begin to apply them in our lives. My prayer is that my personal stories both model manifestation in action, as well as give you a full permission slip to simply be yourself.

MANIFESTED

Module 1

Manifestation Overview

Let Go of Doubt. Set Your Focus.

If you've felt overwhelmed by the vastness of the spiritual space, trust me, you're not alone. Welcome to the club! It can be daunting, incredibly overwhelming, and at times, downright intimidating- speaking from personal experience!

Every piece of knowledge I gain seems to open the door to something else, which used to leave me feeling inadequate. Just a few short years ago, the more I learned, the smaller I felt. It was a cycle that left me spinning, until I found a way to manage it: **focusing on one topic or interest at a time.** That doesn't necessarily mean I turn my eye to learning anything outside of my focus; what I mean is that I choose not to let it deter me from my current path. I have learned to add things to the list of "things I want to learn more deeply one day", instead of getting sidetracked. *(Yes, there is such a list on my phone.)*

I remember putting together the list of manifestations for my 2022 vision board; I wanted to learn and do so much that year, but I knew I had to be meticulous about organizing my desires, as they all contained just too many side streets. I knew I had to reel in my mind and set my *dristi*, the Sanskrit word for focus, on what I *truly* wanted. The following year, I curated my 2023 vision board with ease. I focused solely on energy work, becoming Yin certified, and learning about Europe. Yet, the temptation to explore other areas was always there (such as fascinating subjects like Sacred Geometry, Tarot, Quantum Physics, Religion, and Astrology.) I knew that diving into all of those at once would distract my mind, as well as lower my retention and long-term memory for storing what I had learned.

I am a very methodical person and I have come to adore that part of me. *Do you know your quirks?* I recommend dating yourself and intimately getting to know all "your ways" (for SO many reasons), but mainly so that you can learn how to live authentically and get specific about what you desire! What I've come to learn, is that specificity supports the ability to **focus,** and stay inspired along the manifestation journey.

Suppressing or overlooking any part of who you are will resurface until you learn how to accept and love yourself. So, my advice is to take some time at the beginning of this journey for self-reflection. It will truly support your focus and manifestations in the long run.

Manifestation is not black and white; it's a spectrum *you* create. Although we may share similar foundational tools for manifesting, your unique manifestation techniques and beliefs are completely customizable to who you are as an individual and what you desire. *You may need time to grasp that concept fully, but you'll catch on soon enough.*

To support your process, I've included a glossary at the back of the book to help make sense of some of the terminology I use. While I invite you to read without fixating on understanding every detail of what I've written, feel free to use the glossary as a reference point to create greater clarity on your journey. As you continue reading, please allow the words to wash over you and absorb what resonates with your life *at this moment, the PRESENT*. Remember, we all interpret things differently, depending on where we are in our journey.

I can't emphasize this enough, please invite this book to meet you where you are *now*, and who knows, perhaps when you revisit it in a year, you'll uncover new insights. What doesn't make sense or apply right now, skip it. That's the beauty of growth and learning; it's an ever-evolving process. You don't have to go all-in with everything offered here. It's not all or nothing, so if it starts becoming too much, chill out. Perhaps you just pick "something" to **focus** on for now, and then remember that the other tools are here when you are ready!

Here's to your manifestation journey, wherever it may lead you. As my shaman in Bali once told me, "If you want to discover a deeper understanding of the universe and tap into your greatest gifts, all you have to do is take one spoonful of belief in the possibility of all things unknown to you." So, I did!

What are you waiting on?? Wash away any doubts right now, set your focus, and let's get to MANIFESTING YOUR SHIT!

1.1 Understanding the Law of Attraction

Ever considered how your thoughts might shape your reality? Welcome to the *Law of Attraction,* a powerful principle that suggests, *"Like attracts like."* In essence, the energy you put out into the world draws back experiences that match it.

Think of your thoughts as magnetic forces, actively shaping the contours of your life. Your emotions, those often underestimated drivers, set the tone for the energy you project. It's a dynamic process: the universe responds to your mental and emotional state, aligning events and opportunities with the mindset you carry. By understanding and mastering this connection, you gain the ability to influence the course of your life with greater intention and clarity.

Foundational Principles

1. Thought Power: Consider your thoughts as architects, constructing the blueprint of your reality.

2. Emotional Resonance: Emotions are the painters, adding hues to the canvas of your energy, and influencing the vibrational frequencies you emit.

3. Universal Harmony: Picture the universe as a conductor, orchestrating events in synchrony with your predominant thoughts and feelings.

The Law of Attraction teaches us that when we manifest from a state of joy, love, or happiness, we emit powerful, high-frequency energies that resonate far beyond the vibrations created by lower emotions like shame, worry, or envy.

Science tells us that our bodies are made up of billions of atoms, each carrying a charge (positive, negative, or neutral.) We learned about this in science class as a kid, but personally it didn't make sense to me until now.

Our thoughts and emotions have a significant impact on us at the molecular level. When we dwell in negative emotions like fear or anger, we emit a low frequency, which can lead to attracting situations or experiences that mirror those feelings. For example, if you constantly worry about not having enough money, that anxiety sets a frequency that attracts more financial stress, reinforcing the lack you fear.

"Darkness cannot drive out darkness; only light can do that. Hate cannot drive out hate; only love can do that."

-Dr. Martin Luther King

On the flip side, when we shift our mindset and focus on positive emotions such as gratitude for what we have or excitement about future possibilities, we elevate our energy. This higher frequency attracts opportunities and people that align with that positivity. If you come from an abundant mindset, you will be looking for more blessings. Perception plays a crucial role in this process. How we interpret our experiences can either raise or lower our energetic frequency. Do you ever challenge your thinking? Maybe it is time you start!

The Law of Attraction in History

This isn't a trend-it's history resurfacing again and again...

Ancient Roots:

The roots of the Law of Attraction can be traced to ancient civilizations, where the understanding that thoughts and energies could influence reality was not only acknowledged, but woven into the very fabric of their belief systems.

In ancient Egypt, the concept of *"as within, so without"* echoed through the teachings of Hermes Trismegistus, encapsulating the idea that our inner thoughts and feelings shape our external experiences. Similarly, in ancient China, the Taoist philosophy emphasized the interconnectedness of all things, reflecting the Law of Attraction's core principle of attracting energies aligned with our own

Greek Philosophers and the Power of Mind:

The great minds of ancient Greece discussed the connection between the mind and the world. Plato, Aristotle, and their philosophical contemporaries pondered the idea that the mind holds the power to shape reality. The maxim *"mind over matter"* encapsulated the essence of attracting desired outcomes through the power of thought.

Mysticism in Medieval Times:

As the world transitioned into the medieval era, mystics, and esoteric traditions continued to explore the interplay between consciousness and manifestation. Alchemists sought not only to transmute base metals into gold, but also to unlock the secrets of transforming the self and reality through the alchemy of thoughts and intentions.

The Renaissance and the Emergence of Personal Power:

The Renaissance period witnessed a resurgence of interest in individual empowerment and personal agency. Thinkers like Giordano Bruno and Paracelsus explored the idea that individuals could influence their destinies through the focused power of their minds. The stage was set for the Law of Attraction to become a beacon of personal empowerment.

19th Century New Thought Movement:

The 19th century saw the crystallization of the Law of Attraction into a more systematic philosophy with the emergence of the New Thought movement. Influential figures like Phineas Quimby and Mary Baker Eddy emphasized the role of positive thinking, affirmations, and the power of the mind in shaping one's reality. This era laid the groundwork for the modern understanding of the Law of Attraction.

20th Century Resurgence:

The Law of Attraction experienced a resurgence in the 20th century, finding renewed interest in various forms, from the teachings of Napoleon Hill to the widespread popularity of *"The Secret"* in the early 2000s. This period witnessed a fusion of ancient wisdom, philosophical insights, and contemporary psychology, propelling the Law of Attraction into mainstream consciousness.

Modern-Day Integration:

Today, the Law of Attraction is a cornerstone in the realms of personal development and holistic living. It has transcended cultural and temporal boundaries, becoming a global phenomenon embraced by individuals seeking to manifest positive change in their lives.

In essence, the Law of Attraction is not a New-Age concept but a timeless principle that has resonated through the corridors of history.

Its lasting impact across cultures highlights the universal human desire to understand how our thoughts, energy, and life events are all connected. As we explore its historical roots, we see that manifestation is not merely a new fad of our generation, but a timeless wisdom. This concept has influenced how we create our realities for centuries and continues to do so today.

Key Components of the Law of Attraction

The Law of Attraction operates based on several key components that intertwine to create the force influencing our reality. Understanding these components is crucial for effectively applying the principles of the Law of Attraction.

Here are the key components:

1. Thoughts and Energy:

- Thoughts are not mere fleeting ideas: they are energetic vibrations that radiate from our minds, into our bodies, and then our aura, which emits our frequency into the universe. (We will talk about the science of this soon.)

- Like attracts like: Positive thoughts attract positive energy, while negative thoughts attract negative energy.

- Conscious awareness of our thoughts allows us to intentionally shape the energy we emit.

2. Emotions As Vibrational Signals:

- Emotions are powerful indicators of the vibrational frequency we're emitting.

- Positive emotions, such as joy and love, elevate our energetic state and attract corresponding experiences.

- Negative emotions, like fear and doubt, signal a lower vibrational frequency, attracting circumstances aligned with those feelings.

3. Belief Systems and Subconscious Programming:

- Deep-seated beliefs, often formed during childhood, influence our thoughts and emotions. (I teach this in more detail at my retreats.)

- Our subconscious mind plays a significant role in shaping our beliefs, and these beliefs act as powerful magnets for attracting experiences.

- Identifying and transforming limiting beliefs can enhance the alignment between our conscious desires and our subconscious programming. (Read that again.)

4. Visualization and Imagination:

- Visualization is a technique where we use our imagination to vividly picture our desired outcomes, seeing them as already so.

- Engaging the senses during visualization enhances the emotional resonance, making the manifestation process more potent.

- Regular visualization helps reinforce a positive mindset, and strengthens the connection between thought and reality.

5. Gratitude and Appreciation:

- Gratitude is a high-vibrational emotion that aligns us with positive energies.

- Being grateful for what you currently have creates an atmosphere conducive to abundance.

- Cultivating a daily gratitude practice enhances the overall effectiveness of the Law of Attraction.

6. Inspired Action:

- While the Law of Attraction involves attracting opportunities, taking inspired action is a crucial component.

- Recognizing and acting on opportunities aligned

with your goals reinforces your commitment to the manifestation process.

- Inspired action bridges the gap between visualization and the physical realization of your desires.

7. Detachment and Trust:

- Detachment doesn't mean apathy; it implies maintaining a sense of inner calm and *trust* in the unfolding process.

- Trusting that the universe will respond to your energy and deliver the best possible outcomes is essential. (To me, this is the hardest!)

- Detachment allows you to let go of anxiety and resistance, ultimately creating space for manifestation to naturally occur, due to an increase in your vibration frequency.

8. Alignment with Core Values:

- Manifestation is most effective when your desires align with your core values and authentic self.

- Ensuring that what you seek is in harmony with your true nature enhances the sincerity and power of your manifestations.

- Aligning with your core values fosters a sense of purpose and fulfillment.

By recognizing and integrating these key components, you can enhance your ability to harness the *Law of Attraction*, manifest your desires, and create positive transformations in your life.

1.2 Exploring the Power of Manifestation

Manifestation is more than just wishful thinking; it's a *lifestyle* and belief system with unique, tangible characteristics that make it a transformative practice.

In this section, we explore how adopting manifestation as a way of life can profoundly impact your reality. We delve into the distinct elements that set manifestation apart from mere hope or desire.

Manifestation vs. Wishful Thinking

Manifestation and wishful thinking may seem similar on the surface, both involving desires and hopes for a better future. However, delving into the nuances reveals distinct differences in their nature, processes, and outcomes. Let's uncover these disparities to grasp the true essence of manifestation and understand why it transcends wishful thinking.

1. Clarity of Intention:

- **Manifestation:** In manifestation, there is a clear and specific intention behind the desires. Practitioners articulate their goals with precision, visualizing the details of what they wish to attract into their lives. (You may notice I use the word 'practitioner.' That's because this truly is a *practice*.)

- **Wishful Thinking:** Wishful thinking often lacks explicit clarity. It involves a general desire for something positive to happen without a well-defined plan or vision, leading to no action.

2. Active Engagement:

- **Manifestation:** It is an active and deliberate

process that goes beyond mere longing. Practitioners actively participate in shaping their reality by aligning their thoughts, emotions, and actions with their goals.

- **Wishful Thinking:** Wishful thinking tends to be more passive. Individuals may express a desire for positive outcomes, but they often take no proactive steps toward actualizing their desired outcome.

3. Strategic Planning:

- **Manifestation:** A key aspect of manifestation involves strategic planning and goal-setting. Practitioners identify actionable steps and create a roadmap to bring their desires to fruition.

- **Wishful Thinking:** Wishful thinkers may hope for positive outcomes without a concrete plan. The focus is on the wish itself rather than the practical steps needed to turn it into reality.

4. Energetic Alignment:

- **Manifestation:** Energetic alignment is crucial in manifestation. Practitioners consciously align their thoughts and emotions with the frequency of the desired outcome, creating a harmonious energetic environment. This means seeing it as already so and living as if you already possess what you want or desire.

- **Wishful Thinking:** While positive thinking can be a component of wishful thinking, the energetic alignment may not be as intentional or sustained. Wishful thinking often lacks *the consistent vibrational match* needed for manifestation.

5. Belief and Confidence:

- **Manifestation:** Belief in the possibility of achieving the desired outcome is a core element. Manifestation involves cultivating a *strong* sense of *belief* and confidence in the manifestation process.

- **Wishful Thinking:** Wishful thinkers may harbor *doubts* or uncertainties about the likelihood of their wishes "coming true". The level of belief in the actualization of desires tends to be less robust.

6. Mindset Shift:

- **Manifestation:** It often requires a mindset shift. Practitioners work on transforming limiting beliefs and adopting a positive and empowering mindset aligned with their goals. (reference neuroplasticity in the glossary)

- **Wishful Thinking:** Wishful thinking may occur within existing belief systems, without a deliberate effort to shift perspectives or challenge their beliefs.

When it comes to manifesting your desires, **specificity is key**. Instead of simply stating that you want to lose weight, consider what that means to you. Do you want to reach a certain weight or clothing size? Are you aiming to improve your overall health or fitness level? By clearly defining your goal, you provide the universe with a clear direction on what you want to manifest.

Similarly, rather than vaguely wishing for a dream vacation, take the time to visualize the details. Picture yourself lounging on a sandy beach, exploring a bustling city, or hiking through mountains. Specify the location, activities, duration, and even the budget for your trip this is SO important. The more vividly you can imagine your dream vacation, the more likely you are to bring it to life.

It's important to understand that the universe responds to **clarity** and **intention**. When you can connect senses to your desires such as the ability to imaginatively feel, taste, or smell what you are manifesting, you send a powerful signal to the universe about your desires. On the other hand, if your intentions are vague or uncertain, the universe may struggle to align with your wishes *just as much as you do*! You cannot blame the universe for not delivering exactly what you want when *you* do not know exactly what you want.

So, be specific in your manifestations. Define exactly what you want and why it's important to you. By doing so, *you* empower yourself to *create the life you truly desire.*

In essence, manifestation is a purposeful and proactive approach to turning desires into reality. It involves strategic planning, clarity, and a profound shift in your body and mind.

On the other hand, wishful thinking, while positive, often lacks the intentional and structured elements necessary for successful manifestation.

Understanding these distinctions empowers individuals to move beyond wishful thinking and actively engage in the transformative process of manifestation.

The Impact of Mindset on Manifestation

Thoughts and beliefs are powerful tools that shape your experiences and outcomes. To start improving your mindset, first become aware of your current thought patterns and identify any negative or limiting beliefs you may hold. Be willing to challenge and alter outdated beliefs that no longer serve you. Take a moment to reflect on a belief you strongly hold and ask yourself where it originated. Consider whether this belief truly benefits you or if it was instilled by someone else and might be worth letting go.

In this section, we'll explore practical strategies for cultivating a mindset that aligns with your aspirations. We'll also address how to overcome mental barriers that might be obstructing your manifestation journey. By actively working on your mindset and being open to change, you can pave the way for greater success in realizing your desires.

1. Belief and Expectation:

- Your mindset shapes your beliefs and expectations. If you genuinely believe in the possibility of achieving your goals and maintaining a positive expectation, you are more likely to attract circumstances and opportunities that align with those beliefs.

2. Positive vs. Negative Thinking:

- A positive mindset tends to attract positive outcomes. When you focus on what you want to manifest rather than what you fear or lack, you shift your energy and attention toward opportunities and solutions.

3. Self-Fulfilling Prophecy:

- The self-fulfilling prophecy is a psychological concept where your beliefs about an outcome influence your behavior in a way that brings that outcome to fruition. (I refer to this as the *"Prayer of Gratitude"* or *"The Prayer of Worry"*.)

4. Resilience in the Face of Challenges:

- A confident mindset enhances resilience when facing challenges. Instead of viewing obstacles as insurmountable, individuals with a confident mindset see them as temporary setbacks and opportunities for growth. This resilience is crucial in maintaining momentum toward manifesting goals. (Stay tuned for a personal story on resilience in Module 4, highlighting what I call, 'emotional alchemy'.)

5. Visualization and Affirmations:

- Mindset is closely linked to visualization and affirmations, common tools in the manifestation process. When you consistently visualize your goals as already achieved, and use positive affirmations, you reinforce a mindset that aligns with the reality you wish to create.

6. Emotional Alignment:

- Your emotions are a powerful manifestation tool. A positive mindset generates positive emotions such as joy, gratitude, and enthusiasm. Aligning your emotions with your goals sends a strong signal to the universe and enhances the likelihood of attracting experiences that match your emotional state.

7. Openness to Opportunities:

- A growth-oriented and open mindset encourages exploration and the pursuit of opportunities. When you are open to new possibilities and willing to step outside your comfort zone, you increase the chances of encountering situations that contribute to your goals.

8. Gratitude as a Catalyst:

- Cultivating gratitude is a powerful aspect of mindset in manifestation. Expressing gratitude for what you have and what you are working towards creates a positive energy that supports the attraction of more positive experiences.

9. Mindfulness and Present Moment Awareness:

- A mindful mindset, focused on the present moment, helps you appreciate the journey toward your goals. By staying present and fully engaged in the process, you enhance the manifestation of your desires. It is great to plan or goal-set for the future, but don't overlook the power of the present moment.

Manifestation, to me, is more than just a concept, it's a mindset and a way of life. Once you understand its power and potential, there's no turning back.

Seeing its significant impact on every aspect of life, career, health, finances, relationships, and more, it becomes impossible to go back to navigating life's challenges without intention or purpose. You just won't do it.

Check out a few of my favorite techniques below:

Vision Board: This is an absolute must for me. There's something incredibly gratifying about seeing how closely the reality in which I manifest aligns with what I've visualized and put on my board.

Spelling Words: Words are powerful and they carry energy. Every word you speak is essentially casting a spell over your life. As I reflect, I've been spell-casting my entire life, initially through telling white lies to "fit in" with certain groups in school. However, I've come to realize the positive power of words in manifestation. It's uncanny how the things I speak into existence tend to come true. Affirmations play a similar role here, it's all about the power of words and intention, your brain records the words you speak!

Breathwork: This technique deserves its own book! Whenever I feel myself slipping into a lower frequency (whether it's stress, anger, worry, or grief), I'm not afraid to acknowledge those feelings. I simply take a moment to pause, ask myself why I am feeling this way, and then bring myself back to my breath.

Focusing on my breath helps me quickly return to a state of balance by regulating my nervous system. It's like how my Roomba vacuum knows to go back to its charging stand when it's running low. *"Battery low, return to dock."* You'll notice that your breath is often the first thing you forget about during moments of stress. So, consciously bringing your awareness back to your breath can have many powerful and immediate benefits. The best part, it's FREE!

Give it a try:

Sit comfortably, straighten your posture, roll your shoulders back, relax your jaw, and bring lightness to your face. Take a deep breath in until there's no more room, feel your shoulders rise and your chest expand, and then exhale forcefully, through your mouth, until there's nothing left.

Repeat this a few times and notice the energy shift within you. You might feel it in the tops of your arms or the lightness in your chest. This practice is about learning to work with your body, not against it. I wish schools would teach more about self-awareness and self-regulation like this, rather than some of the less applicable topics we often encounter, but I digress.

In summary, your mindset shapes how you perceive and interact with the world, influencing your actions, emotions, and overall experience. Cultivating a positive, growth-oriented mindset doesn't mean you need to be cheerful all the time (I'm not asking you to ignore your humanity). It's about developing the ability to return to a place where you can view situations differently when needed, ultimately creating greater resiliency along your journey. This mindset helps align your thoughts and beliefs with the reality you aim to create, playing a crucial role in your manifestation process. When you marry your mindset with powerful techniques, such as breathwork or vision boarding, you step into your power as a true co-creator with life.

1.3 Unraveling the Connection Between Thoughts and Reality

As we continue our journey into manifestation mastery, this section delves into the link between our thoughts and the reality we experience. We explore the insights offered by cognitive science, the pivotal role of belief systems, and real-life case studies that illuminate the transformative power of thoughts. This is the part that I thoroughly enjoy. Eeeek. I love science and psychology!!

Cognitive Science and Manifestation

In exploring manifestation, cognitive science provides valuable insights into how our thoughts shape our reality. Here's a look at the key connections between cognitive science and manifestation:

1. Neural Pathways:

Cognitive science (the study of the human mind and brain) shows that our brains create neural pathways based on our habitual thoughts. The older and more entrenched these pathways become, the more complex it can be to reroute them and adopt alternative thinking patterns. Understanding this helps us see how deeply ingrained thoughts can impact our experiences and performance, and why changing these patterns requires deliberate effort.

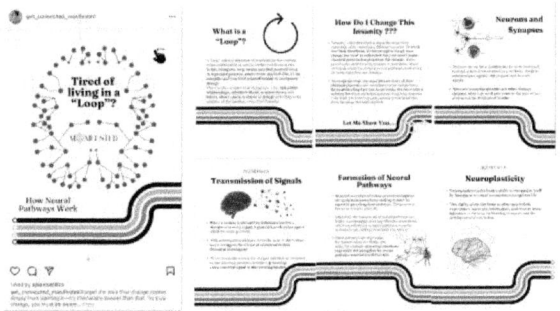

From Brooke's Instagram @get_connected_manifested: A simple look at how neural pathways work.

2. Neuroplasticity:

A fundamental concept in cognitive science, *neuroplasticity*, highlights the brain's ability to adapt and reorganize itself. We possess the ability to rewrite our thoughts by first becoming aware of them as distinct entities and identifying our thinking habits. Once we recognize these patterns, we can intentionally shift them. This adaptability allows us to align our brain's wiring with our desired outcomes through conscious practice.

3. Thought Patterns and Emotions:

Cognitive science explores how thoughts and emotions are deeply interconnected. Thoughts carry emotional *weight* that can amplify their effects. Positive thoughts tend to generate positive emotions, which in turn enhance their influence on our reality. Conversely, negative thoughts trigger lower vibrational frequencies, potentially attracting undesired outcomes. (High vibe=light weight. Low vibe=heavy weight.)

4. Cognitive Biases and Perception:

Exploring cognitive biases reveals how our brains interpret and filter information based on pre-existing beliefs. Manifestation is deeply influenced by these cognitive biases, as our brains selectively attend to information that aligns with our existing thought patterns. Recognizing and addressing cognitive biases allows individuals to reshape their perceptual filters, fostering an environment conducive to intentional manifestation. (See confirmation bias in glossary.)

5. Language and Self-Talk:

Cognitive Linguistics emphasizes how language structures thought. By refining our self- talk and choosing an empowering language, we actively shape the narrative of our experiences. Each word we speak or think contributes to the creation of our reality.

6. Visualization and Neural Coding:

Cognitive Neuroscience underscores the potency of visualization in the manifestation process. When we vividly imagine our desired outcomes, we engage in neural coding – a process where the brain encodes the envisioned scenarios as if they were real experiences. This mental rehearsal strengthens neural connections, enhancing the likelihood of the manifested outcomes as your brain codes the manifestation as already so.

In essence, the marriage of cognitive science and manifestation unveils a captivating synergy where our thoughts, emotions, and neural processes converge to sculpt the reality we inhabit. As we navigate the neural landscape of our minds, we gain the tools to consciously craft our cognitive function and embark on a journey where intentional thoughts become the architects of our experiences. **"Create your reality"**. Are you seeing this, is it resonating? So fun! Okay, let's focus. What's next?

The Role of Belief System

Our beliefs are the foundation that shape how we see and experience the world. When it comes to manifestation, these core beliefs are crucial; they influence our thoughts, affect our emotions, and guide the experiences we bring into our lives, especially in how we react/respond to things. In Module 3 we dive deeper into this subject, but for now, let's break down why our belief systems are so important in the manifestation process.

1. Architects of Reality:

Belief systems are the architects of our reality. They form the lens through which we perceive the world, coloring our experiences and dictating the possibilities we envision. When it comes to manifestation, the alignment of our beliefs with our desired outcomes becomes the cornerstone of intentional creation.

2. Limiting vs. Empowering Beliefs:

The nature of our beliefs determines the course of our manifestation journey. Limiting beliefs, often ingrained from past experiences or external influences, act as constraining forces. They create barriers and hinder the realization of our goals. Conversely, empowering beliefs serve as catalysts, propelling us toward our aspirations and opening pathways to manifestation success.

3. Self-Fulfilling Prophecies:

Beliefs have the remarkable ability to become self-fulfilling prophecies. When we hold a belief, our thoughts and actions align with it, creating a feedback loop that reinforces the belief. This loop, whether positive or negative, becomes a powerful force shaping the unfolding of events and experiences in our lives. (I talk about this "loop" on my Instagram often.)

4. Subconscious Influence:

Many beliefs reside in the subconscious mind, operating *beneath* the surface of conscious awareness. *Which means, you don't know they are there.* Therefore, these subconscious beliefs can exert a profound influence on your thoughts and behaviors. Deciding to do the inner work to uncover and address these beliefs, is a crucial step in aligning your consciousness with your desires for effective manifestation. Without this work, you will literally block yourself from receiving what you dream of.

5. Identifying Limiting Beliefs:

To harness the full potential of manifestation, it's essential to identify and transform limiting beliefs. Through introspection and self-awareness, individuals can pinpoint and replace limiting beliefs with those that support their manifestation goals. (again, neuroplasticity)

6. Affirmations and Belief Reinforcement:

Affirmations act as tools for reshaping belief systems. By consistently repeating positive affirmations aligned with our desired manifestations, we create a counter-narrative to limiting beliefs. This intentional repetition gradually reinforces new, empowering beliefs, paving the way for a shift in thought patterns.

7. Aligning Beliefs with Desires:

Successful manifestation requires a seamless alignment between our beliefs and our desired outcomes. This involves cultivating a mindset that inherently believes in the possibility of achieving goals. The process includes envisioning success, fostering a sense of deservingness, and embracing a belief in the abundance of opportunities.

OUR SURROUNDINGS IMPACT OUR GROWTH

It's crucial to understand that our ability to grow is influenced by our surroundings. Just as a fish can only grow as large as its tank or a flower in a pot, humans are similarly shaped by the environments we find ourselves in.

During an airboat tour in a New Orleans bayou, our guide introduced us to two alligators he had been observing since birth. We fed them, and I even had the opportunity to pet one. The tour was so fun and highly suggested. However, my energy shifted at the end of the tour when our guide revealed a smaller alligator from a small box filled with water, seemingly a mere baby. As I held the tiny creature, he informed our group that it was from the same hatch as the larger ones we had just interacted with in the wild, free. Our guide had kept it as a "boat pet".

Like the alligators, our growth is influenced by our surroundings. While we may encounter limitations, we also have the power to expand our horizons and create environments conducive to our growth. I urge you to not allow others (or your mind) to hold you captive, limiting your growth and abilities.

Our potential grows when we dare to step beyond our comfort zones (or cages). It's crucial to start recognizing the people and situations that may be holding you back. Take a moment to reflect on this. Who comes to mind? Sit with that thought. Do you have an airboat tour guide in your life, stunting your growth or depriving you of swimming in deeper waters?

I was with this little guy, and yes, he was sweet and cute, but he didn't realize what he was missing. He only knew what he had experienced, his little box in an airboat. But look at the vast water behind me, that wide-open, inviting space. This is your sign. Jump in! You're not meant to be confined. You can swim.

OUR SURROUNDINGS IMPACT OUR GROWTH

"You won't know how far you can go until you're no longer limited by where you are."
                              Brooke Coleman

Subconscious Reflection

Our beliefs are often shaped without our awareness, quietly absorbed through experiences and environments rather than intentionally chosen. Take, for example, two households on the same street.

In one home, the parents are extremely wealthy but work long, demanding hours. They return home mentally drained, just wanting to unwind, sip some wine, and be present with their kids. The children, full of energy, bounce on the couch while their parents talk and laugh. There's no concern about the couch getting torn or worn down. It's just a moment of joy, and the parents allow it.

Next door, the situation is different. The father recently lost his job, and the mother stays home to care for the kids. Money is tight. Their couch is old, worn, and irreplaceable. So when their kids start jumping on it, they're scolded immediately. Not because the parents are mean, but because the couch breaking would be a real problem they can't afford. The rule is firm: no jumping on the couch.

As the kids grow up, they carry these rules with them. Not with understanding, but repetition. One household allows jumping, the other doesn't, and the reason why gets lost. It becomes a matter of "we do" or "we don't" without context. The deeper narrative behind the rule fades, and all that's left is behavior, shaped by past circumstances we never paused to examine.

$$\frac{\text{VALUE}}{\text{BELIEF}}$$

This is how beliefs are passed down. Not always with explanation. Not always with context. Often, they're remnants of a past reality, inherited and repeated without ever stopping to ask two crucial questions: Where did this belief originally come from? and Does it still makes sense *now?*

"The dogmas of the quiet past are inadequate to the stormy present."

- Abraham Lincoln

Personal Story

Conditioned Belief, Inherited Fear

The South never truly recovered from losing the Civil War. In many ways, it didn't just pass down recipes, manners, and tradition. It passed down wounds. Cultural trauma is real. Epigenetics tells us that pain can be inherited. Like the famous study where rats exposed to electric shock while smelling lavender passed on the trauma to their future offspring, who had never been shocked, but feared the scent of lavender anyway.

Trauma isn't the only thing we inherit. We also inherit tradition, deeply embedded customs that are often passed down without question. Sayings like "I'll pray for you" or "bless your heart" carry meaning far beyond language. They reinforce a way of thinking rooted in politeness over truth. You're taught to behave, to please, to stay in your place, not to challenge anyone's thinking, not because it's right, but because it's comfortable for everyone else. Be a good little alligator and stay in your box, you feel me?

In the South, we'll hold the door open for you, then become butthurt if you don't mind your manners and say thank you.

Let me explain before you get mad at me.

Southern manners can be beautiful on the surface. We're raised to say *yes ma'am, no sir*, and to keep our voices sweet and low even when something doesn't sit right in our soul. We're taught to perform kindness, not necessarily *embody* it.

I've seen it more times than I can count: someone holds a door, and if the person walking through doesn't respond with instant praise, you'll hear a passive-aggressive "Well, you're welcome." That's not kindness. That's conditioning. *That's ego.*

See, true service doesn't seek applause. If you are holding the door open to be kind for another, you don't need verbal praise- you're simply doing something from a place of true kindness, as a reflection of who and how you are in the world. But when your actions are rooted in needing validation, it exposes something deeper: the difference between real manners and performative control.

To me, Southern manners are often a mask covering up generations of trauma and silent obedience. We confuse politeness with virtue. We confuse obedience with respect. We raise kids to respect elders, even when those elders are emotionally unwell or abusive. We don't teach boundaries. We teach hierarchy. We teach fear.

My mother was a straight-A student. Captain of her high school basketball team. Driven, gifted, and full of dreams. But when she told her father she wanted to go to college, he told her she'd be a whore if she did, and that she'd never be welcome back on the farm. I never met him. He died before I was born. But his shadow lingered and the pain remained.

My mom never told me that story until she was in her 60s. She carried it quietly for decades. But after years of watching me raise my daughters differently, leading them with respect, freedom, and voice she finally opened up. She told me she didn't understand where I got all my "smarts", my mind, my fire. But she admired it.

I told my mother, "You were just as smart as me. You could've been the nurse you always wanted to be. You could've cared for people, like your soul was wired to do. The difference between you and me isn't intelligence, it's *perspective*. It's permission. It's belief."

I'm an Aries. A rebel. A pioneer, at heart. I've always questioned the script. Somewhere along the way, I realized that *belief itself* is powerful, and that perspective creates reality. My ability to question, to reframe, to challenge generational narratives was the beginning of my manifestation journey, even though I didn't know it.

I had been practicing *alchemy* my whole life without even knowing what to call it.

In the South, we don't use words like *alchemy* or *manifestation*. If we did, they'd be dismissed as 'woo woo' and avoided because they threaten the structure of organized control. If people began to spiritually empower themselves, they might start questioning what they were taught. And questioning, around here, makes you dangerous or crazy.

But I was born to shake things up, I have a job to do here. *You do, too, sister!*

Waking Up in The South hasn't been easy.

I know what it's like to be spanked not because I did something terrible, but because my mom was emotionally overwhelmed. My disappointments triggered her and because of her own wounds and conditioning, she didn't know any other way to teach me that I had done something wrong. She didn't have the tools to regulate herself, so she used force. For years I accepted this as normal until one day, I realized that spankings are often a sign of low emotional intelligence. They come from a *reactionary* place of not knowing how to regulate intense emotions such as anger, confusion, or disappointment.

That realization cracked something open in me.

I started remembering things I heard growing up, phrases that were just accepted, even celebrated, without question. Things like, *"They haven't had their ass tore up yet, and that's their problem"*, or *"I brought you into this world, and I'm not afraid to take you out"*. At the time, I stayed silent, because that's what you do. You don't question it. You go along to stay safe.

But now, from the outside looking in, all I can think is: *Wow.* Those weren't jokes. They were signals. Heavy emotions wrapped in humor. Evidence of a culture that glorifies fear and control as discipline, one that equates force with strength.

Once I learned how to hold space for discomfort, I also learned how to hold space for truth. And the truth is: those statements reflect trauma, not toughness. They reveal emotional immaturity being passed off as authority. Instead of teaching our youth how to think, how to lead, or how to emotionally regulate, we've been teaching them how to submit. How to bow to control.

Then we wonder why the South is so poor, while the money and innovation are in the North, the Midwest, and the West. It's because the South isn't raising visionaries. It's raising laborers and limited minds.

When my daughters were young, my husband and I hosted an au pair from Sweden. In the beginning I judged her ways. Her softness. Her calm pace. Her parenting insights. I thought, *They're so lax over there. Where's the discipline?*

After four months of watching how she moved with my children, I saw something I hadn't expected. I saw patience that had been modeled for generations before her. I saw emotional calm passed down through her culture. I saw children being guided, not controlled. For the first time, I thought: *Maybe there's another way.* Although she was only with our family for one short year, I know God placed her in my life to help me begin to *see* in a different way. I don't believe in coincidences. She was truly a gateway for me, and I never parented my kids the same afterwards.

Being born in the South, however, you inherit fear, pride, and the pressure to perform. You inherit rituals without roots, ideologies masked as manners, and the same close-minded, quick-to-judge, opinionated thinking patterns that were passed down as truth. Instead of teaching emotional intelligence, we inherited reactive patterns. Instead of curiosity, we inherited conformity.

Waking up means unlearning. *Re-seeing.* When beliefs are tied to God, country, or family, it's a painful undoing. Let me explain what I mean here-

And when he was demanded of the Pharisees, when the
kingdom of God should come, he answered them and
said, The kingdom of God cometh not with
observation: Behold, the kingdom of God is within you.
-Luke 17:20–21 (KJV)

When the Pharisees asked Jesus when the Kingdom of God would come, they were expecting an external sign, something to appear in the sky, a revolution, a throne. Jesus shattered their assumptions with a simple, powerful truth: the Kingdom is not out there somewhere. It is within you. This moment is more than theological. It's an invitation to remember who you are. You don't need to chase God, prove yourself to others, or perform your way into worthiness. You were never meant to search outside, your identity is not "out there", your identity is within. To faithfully serve any religion at all you must serve it as YOU.

As you digest the content of Module 1 you may be confronted with your own undoing. For some of you this might be exciting. You feel ready to break through old ways of being and create new ones. For others this might feel unexpectedly uncomfortable or confusing. For a lot of you, it'll feel like a little bit of both. That's ok. There's no right or wrong way to begin this journey, and it's certainly not a race. Slow down. Take your time. Remain curious. There are lots of tools in the next Module to support whatever thoughts or emotions are coming up for you. Additionally, the journal prompt provided on the next page is a great place to start!

Journal Entry

Mirrored Reflection

Find a quiet, comfortable space where you can sit undisturbed in front of a mirror. Take a few deep breaths to center yourself. Soften your gaze and allow your thoughts to settle as you look into your own eyes through the mirror's reflection.

What is your first impression as you gaze at the person looking back at you? Do you feel shocked, pleased, or something else entirely? Take a few moments to simply witness yourself without judgment or criticism.

Now go deeper. Do you like what you see? If not, what is it that you dislike or wish to change about your appearance or the person you perceive yourself to be? Where did this self-criticism or belief originate? Can you pinpoint when these **beliefs** first took root? What was that time like for you?

Whose voices have you internalized and adopted as your own? Are they echoes of past criticism from others or tapes you replay in your own mind? Is there a cheerleader in there too? Take some time to explore the origin of these limiting perceptions or positive influences and how they came to be.

If thoughts of self-judgment or criticism arise, do not resist them. Instead, acknowledge their presence with curiosity, allowing them to rise and pass like clouds in the sky. You do not need to attach to them or make them part of your identity but it is necessary to bring awareness to them, knowing they are there

Once you have sat with this process for a while, take out your journal. Record any revelations, patterns, or sources of negativity that you uncovered during this exercise. Let the words flow without filtering. Now do you see you?

When you have fully emptied your observations onto the page, return your gaze to the mirror. This time, ask yourself , "If I cannot see and accept the beauty, light, and spirit within myself, how can I expect others to perceive my true essence?".

What small shift might allow you to soften into self-acceptance? Is it possible to have compassion for the human journey of struggle you have walked? See if you can offer that person in the mirror the loving-kindness they deserve.

Close with a few final deep breaths, sealing your intention to develop a kinder, more nurturing inner voice and relationship with your most authentic self.

MANIFESTED

Module 2

Setting the Stage for Your Manifestation Practice

2.1 Meditation for Manifestation

Meditation is the space where the power of manifestation meets mindfulness, where you truly connect with yourself. In this section, we'll explore how to create your own meditation space, use visualization techniques to boost your manifestations, and introduce you to guided meditation. If you've never meditated before, no worries, it's all about starting where you are! And hey, don't be the alligator or a naysayer, remember, we're rewiring your thinking here, right?!

Creating a Conducive Meditation Space

Creating a peaceful meditation space is essential for decluttering your mind. This sacred space serves as the foundation for your inner journey, enhancing your focus, serenity, and alignment with the energies of manifestation. Whether religious or not, you can think of this space like your own personal temple or church.

Here's a guide to help you create an environment that nurtures your meditation experience: .

1. Select a Quiet Location:

- Choose a space where you can find tranquility and minimize external disturbances.

- Opt for a quiet room or a corner in a room, away from the hustle and bustle of daily activities.

2. Adjust Lighting:

- Natural light is ideal, but if that's not possible, opt for soft, diffused lighting.

- Consider using candles, Himalayan salt lamps, or dimmable artificial lights to create a serene ambiance.

3. Comfortable Seating:

- Select a comfortable seat or cushion. You can choose a meditation cushion, a chair with good back support, or a folded blanket.

- Ensure your posture allows you to sit comfortably with a straight spine, promoting alertness and relaxation.

4. Set the Temperature:

- Maintain a comfortable room temperature. If possible, use blankets or shawls to ensure warmth during meditation.

- Avoid extremes in temperature that might distract you during your practice.

5. Declutter the Space:

- Keep the meditation area clutter-free to minimize distractions.

- Remove unnecessary items and create a simple, serene environment that fosters a sense of calm.

6. Incorporate Nature Elements:

- Introduce elements of nature, such as indoor plants, to bring a sense of grounding and connection to the outdoors.

7. Personalize with Meaningful Items:

- Place meaningful items in your meditation space, such as crystals, spiritual or religious symbols, or objects that hold personal significance or dear to your heart.

- These items can serve as anchors for positive energy and intention.

8. Consider Scents:

- Use essential oils, incense, or scented candles to introduce calming scents.

Examples of Calming Scents:

Lavender: *Lavender is perhaps one of the most well-known calming scents. Its gentle floral aroma has been shown to reduce stress and anxiety, promote relaxation, and improve sleep quality.*

Chamomile: *Chamomile has a soothing, herbal scent that is often associated with relaxation and tranquility. It is commonly used in aromatherapy to promote calmness and alleviate stress.*

Sandalwood: *Sandalwood has a warm, woody aroma that is known for its grounding and calming properties. It can help induce a sense of inner peace and relaxation.*

Bergamot: *Bergamot has a citrusy, floral scent with subtle spicy undertones. It is often used in aromatherapy to uplift the mood, reduce stress, and promote relaxation.*

Ylang Ylang: *Ylang Ylang has a sweet, floral scent that is often described as exotic and sensual. It is known for its calming and mood-boosting properties, making it a popular choice for relaxation.*

Frankincense: *Frankincense has a rich, resinous aroma with earthy and woody notes. It is revered for its grounding and meditative qualities, making it ideal for promoting relaxation and spiritual connection.*

- Choose fragrances that resonate with you and evoke positive emotion.

9. Create a Meditation Altar:

- If space allows, consider creating a small meditation altar.

- Arrange items symbolizing your spiritual or personal journey, adding a focal point for your practice.

A **meditation altar** is a sacred space or area set up specifically for the practice of reflection, worship, contemplation, prayer, or spiritual rituals. It can be personalized to reflect one's beliefs, intentions, and aesthetic preferences.

A meditation altar typically includes objects and items that hold personal significance or symbolic meaning.

These may include:

- Images or statues of deities, religious figures, or symbols representing higher powers or beliefs.

- Candles or incense to create a serene atmosphere and aid in concentration.

- Crystals, stones, or gemstones believed to have specific energetic properties or spiritual significance.

- Inspirational quotes, affirmations, or sacred texts to provide guidance and inspiration.

- Natural elements such as flowers, plants, or shells

to evoke a sense of connection to the earth and the natural world.

- Tarot and Oracle Cards:

  - Keeping a deck of Tarot or Oracle cards at your meditation altar can be a powerful tool on days when you feel like you need more than simply sitting and breathing or visualizing.

  - Pulling cards can be a great way to externalize your practice, which is especially supportive for those of us who are visual or kinesthetic learners. Just seeing an image outside of yourself could help you access your intuition on a whole new level!

  - The physical ritual of setting an intention, shuffling the cards, and then intuitively pulling what cards you feel drawn to, can be very grounding for the nervous system-ultimately allowing you to access your higher self more easily.

  - Depending on your belief system, you may view these tools as witchcraft. If so, I totally honor and respect that. However, at its core, Tarot is a system designed as a universal tool to help you access your internal dialogue through symbols and images. It draws from the subconscious mind and brings buried thoughts or truths to the surface for the conscious mind to process and reflect.

- Despite was social media trends say, Tarot or Oracle cards aren't about predicting the future. These ancient divination systems are actually about tuning into what already lives within us and gives it the space to be seen.

- Once we see the unseen, we may feel empowered to make new choices in our lives, which yes, does alter our future. But make no mistake, it's *us* making the choices, not the cards. The cards just reveal what we already knew and are now giving ourselves permission to know.

During my awakening journey, I took the time to formally study and understand Tarot. I came to deeply appreciate the clarity and insight it offers. Anyone can read Tarot, regardless of language or culture. So, I truly see this as a beautiful system for connection-both with self, and a global community of others on the path of transformation. If you are new to the cards, go slow, have fun, and know that there's no right or wrong way to engage with them. Your practice, is *yours*.

Example of a Meditation Altar

The arrangement and composition of meditation altars are highly individualized and can vary widely depending on your beliefs, cultural background, and spiritual/religious path. The altar serves as a tangible representation of one's journey and a space for quiet reflection, introspection, and connection with the divine.

10. Digital Detox:

- Turn off electronic devices or set them to silent mode to avoid interruptions.

- Create a space free from digital distractions, allowing you to fully immerse yourself in the present moment.

11. Soft Background Music or Sounds:

- Optionally, include soft background music, nature sounds, or meditation music. Certain frequencies can help create a conducive environment for manifestation by influencing mood, relaxation, focus, and mental clarity. Here are a few frequencies that some individuals associate with manifesting or enhancing various aspects of consciousness:

    - **432 Hz:** Often referred to as the *"miracle tone"* or *"healing frequency,"* 432 Hz is believed by some to have a calming and harmonizing effect on the body and mind. It is thought to resonate with nature and promote a sense of well-being.

    - **528 Hz:** Known as the *"love frequency,"* 528 Hz is believed to facilitate healing, promote DNA repair, and evoke feelings of love, compassion, and positivity. Some people use this frequency for manifesting intentions related to abundance, health, and relationships.

    - **639 Hz:** This frequency is **associated with harmonious interpersonal relationships,** forgiveness, and emotional healing.** It is believed to enhance communication, foster connection, and promote reconciliation.

- **741 Hz:** Often referred to as the *"frequency of consciousness expansion,"* 741 Hz is believed to stimulate intuition, enhance problem-solving abilities, and facilitate self-expression. It is associated with creativity, clarity, and inner wisdom.

- **852 Hz:** This frequency is thought to **promote spiritual enlightenment, intuition, and inner peace.** It is believed to awaken intuition, enhance spiritual awareness, and facilitate access to higher states of consciousness.

NOTE- Ensure the soundscape you choose enhances the meditation experience without becoming a distraction.

12. Maintain Cleanliness:

- Keep your meditation space clean and well-maintained.

- Regularly dust, vacuum, and refresh the space to create a harmonious and inviting atmosphere.

By dedicating time and attention to creating a personal meditation space, you're setting up a place that *feels* uniquely yours; just like how some men love their man-caves and women cherish their powder rooms or vanities. There's something inspiring about being in "our space", a spot where you can truly be yourself and express yourself. This sanctuary becomes a reflection of your commitment to self-discovery, inner peace, and intentional manifestation. As you step into this space, let it be a haven where your mind finds stillness, your heart finds peace, and your spirit taps into the endless possibilities within you.

Visualization Techniques During Meditation

Visualization is a potent tool that transforms the abstract into the concrete, turning aspirations into tangible realities. In the realm of meditation, visualization becomes a dynamic force, guiding the mind to paint vivid images that align with your desires.

Let's explore visualization techniques

1. Create a Mental Canvas:

- Begin by envisioning a blank canvas in your mind's eye. (Close your eyes and see within.) This blank canvas symbolizes the limitless space where your thoughts can be created. Ready to paint?

2. Picture Specific Details:

- Choose a specific goal or desire you wish to manifest and bring it to the forefront of your mind.

- Visualize the details with clarity – colors, shapes, textures, and any other specific features associated with your goal. *Example: If you're manifesting a trip, picture the destination, people, events, or the sights.*

3. Engage Your Senses:

- Immerse yourself in the visualization by engaging your senses. Feel the texture, smell the scents, and hear the sounds associated with your desired outcome.

- The more senses you involve, the more vivid and real the visualization becomes-creating a greater bond of synapses in your brain.

4. Integrate Emotions:

- Connect with the emotions tied to your desired manifestation. Feel the joy, gratitude, and fulfillment as if your goal has already been achieved.

- Emotions are the catalysts that infuse your visualization with a powerful energetic resonance.

5. Dynamic Imagery:

- Allow the images on your canvas to be dynamic and fluid. See the progression from the present moment to the realization of your goal.

- Visualize the journey as if you are replaying a memory.

- Play the entire scenario out in your head as you just witnessed it on a YouTube short.

6. Personalize Your Visualization:

- Make the visualization deeply personal. See yourself actively participating in the realization of your goal ***and how you feel.***

- Incorporate images of yourself accomplishing tasks, interacting with others, and fully experiencing the positive outcomes.

- Is your hair short or long, are you laughing or

eating, what does the weather feel like on your face, can you hear your laughter?

7. Repetition and Consistency:

- Practice your visualization regularly. Repetition reinforces the neural pathways associated with your desired manifestation.

- Consistent visualization deepens the connection between your thoughts, emotions, and the energetic frequencies you emit.

8. Expand Beyond the Immediate Goal:

- While focusing on your immediate goal, expand your visualization to encompass the ripple effects on other aspects of your life.

- See how the manifestation positively influences your relationships, well-being, and overall sense of fulfillment.

9. Create a Visualization Ritual (Routine):

- Develop a ritual around your visualization practice. Whether it's a specific time of day, a dedicated meditation space, or incorporating certain scents or music, establish a routine that enhances the potency of your visualizations.

10. Express Gratitude:

- Conclude your visualization with a sense of gratitude. Express thanks for the manifestations already set in motion and trust in the unfolding journey. That everything your heart desires is yours.

Visualization during meditation is a transformative practice that bridges the gap between intention and reality. By vividly imagining your desired outcomes, you actively participate in the co-creation of your future. As you refine your visualization techniques, allow the images on your canvas to be a source of inspiration, motivation, and a constant reminder of the incredible power within you.

2.2 Mindfulness Practices to Enhance Focus

While visualization techniques are a powerful part of manifestation, helping you connect with your future self and align energetically with your desires, it's equally important learn how to ground yourself in the present moment.

Manifestation isn't just about imagining what could be; it's about embodying the energy of it *now*. That's where mindfulness comes in.

Mindfulness is much different than visualization, but an equally powerful practice that involves being fully present and engaged in the current moment.

This section will explore various mindfulness practices to improve concentration and clarity of thought.

Techniques for Staying Present

1. Mindful Breathing:

- Center your attention on your breath, considering it as an anchor.

- Notice each inhale and exhale, acknowledging the energy and intention you breathe in and out.

- If your mind wanders, gently bring your attention back to your breath, realigning with a natural and calming flow.

2. Observe Your Surroundings

- Engage your senses with purpose. Take a moment to observe your surroundings and draw in your senses. What do you smell, hear, see, and feel right here, right now? I normally set a 5 minute timer for this. By the end of 5 minutes I have found so much!

- This practice keeps you grounded in the present moment.

3. Mindful Walking:

- Incorporate mindful walking into your manifestation practice.

- With each step, envision yourself moving closer to your desired manifestations.

4. Use of Mantras or Affirmations:

- Choose mantras or affirmations that align with your specific manifestations.

- Repeat these words with conviction, letting them become powerful focal points.

- "I AM" is a great mantra to start to work with.

5. Cultivate Gratitude:

- Reflect on what you're grateful for in the present moment, channeling positive energy into your desires, then state it out loud.

6. Self Acceptance:

- Accept where you are right now as the starting point for your journey.

- Acknowledge your thoughts and feelings. Accept them without criticism, understanding they are part of your path.

- Practice non-judgment. Foster a positive and accepting mindset to support your manifestation goals.

Mindful Breathing Exercise

Mindful breathing is a powerful tool for calming the nervous system, leading to a lighter, freer energy and life.

Here's why:

When you breathe mindfully, focusing on slow, deep breaths, you activate the parasympathetic nervous system, which is the "rest and digest" part of your autonomic nervous system. This system counteracts the "fight or flight" response triggered by the sympathetic nervous system, which is often overactive in our fast-paced, stress-filled lives.

By consciously controlling your breath, you slow down your heart rate, lower blood pressure, and reduce the levels of stress hormones like cortisol. This shift not only relaxes the body but also soothes the mind, creating a sense of inner calm.

As your nervous system settles, you become more present and aware, freeing your energy from the tensions of past worries or future anxieties. This presence allows your energy to flow more freely, unburdened by the physical and mental stresses that often weigh it down. As a result, life feels lighter, and you experience a greater sense of freedom, both mentally and emotionally.

In essence, mindful breathing reconnects you to a state of balance, where your energy can expand and your life can unfold with greater ease and lightness.

Let's cover a few options for this practice:

1. Diaphragmatic Breathing for Manifestation:

- Find a comfortable seated position, place one hand on your chest and the other on your abdomen.

- Inhale deeply through your nose, allow your abdomen to expand while keeping your chest relatively still.

- Exhale slowly through pursed lips, feel your abdomen contract.

- Visualize inhaling the energy of your manifestations and exhaling any doubts or resistance.

2. Counted Breaths Manifestation Technique:

- Sit in a quiet space and close your eyes.

- Inhale slowly to the count of six and exhale for six counts.

- Gradually increase the count as you become more comfortable.

- With each inhale, visualize manifesting your goals, and on the exhale, release any tension or obstacles.

3. Breath Awareness and Manifestation:

- Sit or lie down in a relaxed position, focus your attention on the natural rhythm of your breath.

- Notice the sensation of air entering and leaving your body. As thoughts arise, gently bring your focus back to your breath.

- Infuse each breath with the intention of manifesting your desires.

4. Box Breathing Manifestation Ritual: (this is my favorite)

- Inhale deeply for a count of four, hold your breath for four counts, exhale for a count of four, and then pause for another four counts before inhaling again.

- Infuse each breath with the intention of manifesting your desires.

5. Alternate Nostril Breathing for Manifestation:

- Sit comfortably with a straight spine.

- Use your thumb and ring finger to alternately block one nostril at a time.

- Inhale through one nostril, visualize your manifestation goals, then exhale through the other nostril.

- Repeat, alternating nostrils, and maintain a clear focus on your intentions.

Credits: The Chalkboard Mag

Nostril breathing, especially techniques like Nadi Shodhana (alternate nostril breathing), can enhance manifestation practices due to its benefits for the mind, body, and energy system.

Here's why nostril breathing supports manifestation:

1. **Balancing Energy Channels:** Nostril breathing techniques, like *Nadi Shodhana*, are thought to

balance the energy flow through the *nadis* (subtle energy channels) in your body. By harmonizing the *Ida* and *Pingala nadis*, associated with the left and right nostrils, respectively, you may achieve greater internal alignment.

2. **Calming the Mind:** Nostril breathing practices calm the mind and nervous system, reducing stress, anxiety, and mental agitation. This creates a more favorable internal environment for setting intentions and manifesting desires. A relaxed and focused mind can better concentrate on goals and visualize outcomes with clarity and intention.

3. **Enhancing Focus and Concentration:** Nostril breathing techniques enhance focus, concentration, and mental clarity. By regulating your breath and focusing on its flow, you develop mindfulness and present-moment awareness, which are crucial for effective manifestation. Improved focus helps you direct your thoughts and energy toward your desires or goals with greater precision and intensity.

4. **Promoting Relaxation and Receptivity:** Nostril breathing promotes relaxation and receptivity, helping you enter a more open state of consciousness. In this relaxed state, your subcon-

scious mind becomes more accessible, making it easier to plant intentions and influence the subconscious programming that shapes your reality. Manifestation is more effective when your intentions are deeply rooted in the subconscious mind.

5. **Aligning with Universal Flow:** Some practitioners find that nostril breathing aligns your energy with the universal flow of *prana* or life force energy. By harmonizing your internal energy with this universal energy, you might experience greater synchronicities, opportunities, and manifestations in your life.

2.3 Visualization Mastery

Just like in art class, when you carefully chose each macaroni noodle or dab of glitter glue, creating a vision board is all about selecting the images, words, and symbols that resonate with your heart's desires.

This isn't just an exercise in creativity, it's a powerful manifestation tool backed by science. When you visualize, your brain processes the images as if they are real, activating the same neural pathways used during actual experiences. This process enhances your ability to manifest by aligning your thoughts and energy with your goals.

So, grab your magazines, scissors, and glue sticks, it's time to create proof of your dreams on paper, just like those cherished art class projects you were so proud of.

Creating Vision Boards

1. Set Your Intentions:

- Clarify your manifestation goals and intentions before starting the vision board creation process.

- Consider the specific areas of your life, relationships, career, health, and define what success looks like for each.

2. Gather Materials:

- Collect magazines, images, quotes, and any other materials that resonate with your goals.

- Include colors, textures, and elements that evoke

positive emotions and visually represent your desires.

3. Create a Sacred Space:

- Choose a quiet and comfortable space where you can focus without distractions, *perhaps your meditation alter or space?*

- Play calming music or light candles to create a serene atmosphere conducive to the manifestation process.

4. Selection and Arrangement:

- Select images and words that align with your visualized goals.

- Arrange these elements on a board in a way that feels visually harmonious and resonates with your intentions.

- Trust your intuition during this process; there are no strict rules let your creativity flow and let any OCD go!!! Perfectionism is ego and ego doesn't thrive here. It isn't invited.

5. Affirmations and Quotes:

- Integrate your chosen affirmations and motivational quotes that reinforce your beliefs in achieving your goals.

- These affirmations serve as constant reminders of your capability to manifest and succeed.

6. Personal Touch:

- Include personal photos or items that hold sentimental value and are connected to your goals. This personal touch adds a layer of authenticity to your vision board, strengthening its manifestation power.

7. Display Your Vision Board:

- Place your completed vision board where you will see it daily.

- Choose a spot that allows you to reflect on your goals daily. It doesn't have to be anywhere fancy, just somewhere you'll see it often. Mine, for example, is right in front of my toilet (sorry if that's TMI!). But hey, it's a place where I can't ignore it, and that's the point. The more you see your vision board, the more those images and goals will embed into your subconscious, fueling your manifestation journey.

8. Periodic Updates:

- As your goals evolve, revisit and update your vision board.

- Add new elements or adjust existing ones to reflect your changing aspirations and desires.

Creating a vision board is a dynamic and ongoing process. It serves as a tangible manifestation tool, reminding you of your goals and reinforcing your commitment to journey

By infusing your vision board with intention, creativity, and personal touches, you are actively participating in the manifestation process, bringing your dreams into the realm of reality.

And for my logical, linear type thinkers- Yes, you are correct in your thoughts right now, this technique works because you are constantly reminding yourself of your vision by it simply being in front of you. That is definitely what I am saying. This technique works incredibly well for goal-setting, career-focused individuals because of just that.

"So, manifestation is goal setting?" Now you are getting it!! Manifestation is NOT magic- YOU are! Take a look at the vision board below and imagine what yours will look like.

Example of a Vision Board

The Science Behind Visualization and Manifestation

As I mentioned, manifestation is not magic. Visualization is not just a whimsical exercise; it's grounded in scientific principles that have a profound impact on our brains and, consequently, our reality. I've listed a few important connections below.

Neuroplasticity - Rewiring the Brain:

- Our brains possess an incredible capacity for change, known as *neuroplasticity.*

- When we engage in visualization, we stimulate neural pathways associated with the imagined actions, essentially rewiring the brain to align with our manifested goals.

- This process strengthens the belief in our ability to achieve those goals, creating a neural blueprint for success.

Reticular Activating System (RAS) - Focusing the Mind:

- The Reticular Activating System (RAS) acts as a filter, determining which information our brain prioritizes.

- Visualization, when consistently practiced, instructs the RAS to recognize and amplify elements related to our manifested goals.

- This heightened awareness makes us more attuned to opportunities, resources, and connections that align with our visualized outcomes.

Emotional Brain Response - Feeling the Manifestation:

- Positive emotional engagement during visualization triggers a biochemical response, releasing neurotransmitters that reinforce our belief in the possibility of manifestation.

Mirror Neurons - Bridging Imagination and Reality:

- Mirror neurons in the brain fire both when we perform an action and when we observe someone else performing that action.

Psychoneuroimmunology (PNI) - Mind-Body Connection:

- A field of study that explores the interactions between the mind (psycho), the nervous system (neuro), and the immune system (immunology). *It's all connected.*

- Positive visualization has been linked to a strengthening of the immune system and overall well-being.

- This connection between mind and body underscores that our mental state strongly affects our physical health, thereby influencing our capacity to manifest. It scrutinizes the impact of psychological factors such as thoughts, emotions, beliefs, and behaviors, on immune system functionality and overall health.

Quantum Physics - Observer Effect:

- Quantum physics introduces the concept of the observer effect, suggesting that the act of observation alters the behavior of particles.

- In the context of manifestation, our focused attention and intention during visualization may influence the energy around us, affecting the outcome of events in our favor.

Idealism

- Is a philosophical perspective that posits the primacy of ideas, thoughts, or consciousness in shaping and defining reality.

- In essence, it suggests that reality is fundamentally mental or conceptual in nature, rather than being entirely independent of the mind.

There are various forms of idealism, but they generally share the belief that the external world, including physical objects and events, is dependent on the mind or consciousness for its existence or nature to be known. Here are some key aspects of idealism:

1. **Primacy of Mind:** Idealism asserts that the mind or consciousness is primary and that everything we experience or perceive is ultimately a product of mental phenomena.

2. **Subjective Reality:** Idealism suggests that reality is subjective and can vary depending on the perspective or consciousness of the observer. According to this view, there is no objective reality that exists independently of subjective experience.

3. **Representation:** Idealists often argue that what we perceive as the external world is actually a representation or projection of mental phenomena. In other words, our perceptions of the world are shaped by our mental faculties and conceptual frameworks.

Understanding the science and philosophy behind visualization empowers us to approach this practice with a sense of grounded optimism. It reinforces that visualization is not just wishful thinking; it's a dynamic process that actively shapes our neural landscape, perceptions, and ultimately, our manifested reality. As we explore the depths of visualization mastery, let this scientific foundation be a source of confidence in the potency of our mind's creative potential.

BE HERE NOW

Through creating a sacred space for your practice, and using many of the techniques discussed in this module, you are giving yourself the gift of *presence.* This gift sounds great, but can often be the most challenging aspect to the manifestation process. So many of us unconsciously operate on autopilot, repeating thoughts about the past or worried about the future. Manifestation, however, happens in the present moment, which is truly the only moment we really have.

Delving into your past is unnecessary, except when it surfaces in your current thoughts, emotions, or experiences, thus impacting your present moment. Your present challenges will always reveal what you need to know about your past. But, believing that understanding your past will free you, is a delusion.

Gaining insights from the past can be valuable, but it's not essential. Remember, you aren't the same person you were back then. Your perception of past events was shaped by who you were at the time, not who you are now. What's crucial is your conscious presence today.

Many people endlessly analyze their past, thinking that if they can just understand why something happened, they'll find peace. While therapy may be necessary for some, many can find the peace they seek simply by being present.

To truly understand presence, you must experience it. When you wash dishes, feel the warmth of the water on your hands, and the scent of the soap. Don't rush through it as just another task. Instead, see it as a moment of aliveness.

Let's try an experiment. Close your eyes and ask yourself, "I wonder what my next thought will be." Then, become very alert and wait for the next thought to appear. Be like a cat watching a mouse hole, ready to pounce on whatever comes out. Try it now! What happened? Was your next thought, the thought of looking for your next thought itself? See how you can do that, control your thinking by directing your thoughts to your next thought subconsciously. Mmmmm.

"You weren't born with your beliefs. You inherited them."

PERSONAL STORY

FROM CONVICTION TO CONNECTION

Before religion became a performance, a system, or a political tool, it was something sacred. A sin wasn't something meant to convict or guilt you into submission. It wasn't designed to keep you afraid. It was an invitation to course correct, to return to your truest self. A "sin", in its original essence, wasn't meant to condemn you to eternal punishment. It was simply a behavior, a pattern, or a choice that pulled you away from wholeness, away from your highest self. Sin was anything that confined your spirit, made you sick, dimmed your light, or dulled your joy.

In fact, the word *sin* in ancient Hebrew, **ḥāṭā'**, literally meant "to miss the mark", like an archer missing their target. It was about straying from alignment with your true purpose. Not something others could wield against you, but your own internal knowing, a compass designed to help you recalibrate and return home to your truth.

And if you think about it, that's exactly how manifestation works.

When you "miss the mark," you're not being punished, you're being shown where you're out of alignment. You're being invited to course correct your thoughts, your energy, your patterns, your perception. You can't attract peace while sitting in a state of war with yourself. You can't manifest love while broadcasting hate. Alignment matters.

Just like you're witnessing teens today give new meanings to words, history has done the same thing over and over again. Traditionally, "slay" meant to kill or destroy; it had serious and violent connotations. But now? "She slayed that performance," which has extremely positive connotations. The word evolved, just like how the spiritual meaning of "sin" has morphed through mistranslation and misuse.

Words evolve. So do thoughts. So do you.

But here's the trap: we cling so tightly to today's understanding of religious language, as if it's always been that way. We forget that words like sin, salvation, and even God have been shaped by centuries of translation, politics, cultural bias, and social conditioning. And we wonder why we feel disconnected.

The danger isn't in questioning these words, it's in *not* questioning them.

Most people don't know that early Christians, like Origen, described sin not as a crime, but as a *spiritual illness;* not something to be shamed for, but healed from. Just like a poor diet makes the body sluggish, unaligned choices make the soul sick. The more we stay in low-frequency emotions, shame, guilt, fear, or envy, the more we "miss the mark." The more we disconnect from the energetic alignment needed for manifestation, healing, and clarity.

Lying creates spirals of shame. Envy distracts us from gratitude. Gluttony burdens the body and slows our vibration. Alcohol raises cortisol and clouds our clarity. These aren't punishments, they're frequencies. Everything is energy. And the energy we embody becomes the reality we attract. That's not just spiritual, it's science, it's neuroplasticity, it's manifestation.

Sin was once your compass. Today, that compass has been hijacked by shame, control, and conformity. Our connection to God was replaced with hierarchy. Our connection to self stripped away. When you disconnect from yourself, you disconnect from your power to manifest. You can't attract what you don't believe you're worthy of. You can't create a life of joy if you've been conditioned to believe you don't deserve it.

Even the idea of the *temple* has shifted.

Ancient cultures, from Egyptian to Hindu to Greek, treated temples as sanctuaries of healing. Spaces full of sacred geometry, incense, gardens, and silence. These weren't places to be seen. They were places to return to stillness, to recalibrate energy, to align intention with divinity. Temples were energetic tuning forks. Today, science calls that coherence, the harmony between heart, brain, and body. That's when manifestation becomes *magnetic.*

But down here, preachers have taken over the temples.

Stillness has been replaced by sermons. Healing replaced by hierarchy. Silence replaced by performance. The temple has been turned into a stage. If you miss a Sunday, shame on you, "the Lord don't like that". If you ask a question, you are told to just "have faith" because to question anything is a 'sin". Of course it is, how fitting to create a rule that guilts us for having a brain instead of celebrating our capacity for curiosity and learning. Even passages of the Bible are interpreted and taught misleadingly from its context in order to use it as a form of control instead of a loving connection to the Divine.

In Catholicism, the ritual of confession holds more value than conviction. It's about letting the soul breathe, releasing guilt instead of suppressing it. But modern Christianity? It's about suppressing the wound, spraying it down with hairspray, and smiling through your lipstick painted teeth. Performance is easier than presence. But the nervous system doesn't lie. Suppression creates dis-ease. Alignment, truth, and honesty, that's where the nervous system resets. That's where healing begins. That's where the brain starts to rewire, and manifestation begins to flow again.

In America, nearly 70% of the population identifies as Christian, yet antidepressant usage is among the highest in the world. That's not a coincidence. In Eastern cultures, where spiritual practice is more internal, people sit with their pain, meditate through it, honor the ancestors, reconnect with source. They don't run from discomfort; they breathe through it. In America, we suppress and call it salvation. But suppressed pain is stored pain. And stored pain keeps you from manifesting your highest life in so many ways.

Church isn't where I found healing. It's where I learned to hide.

I remember questioning everything I was taught. The guilt, the fear, the internal war of wanting to feel free but being told that freedom was sin. I thought I was breaking up with Jesus, and it was killing me. But it wasn't Him I needed to leave; it was the version of Him they handed me in the pew. A version filtered through fear, patriarchy, and ego.

I began to WAKE UP.

Traveling. Questioning. Exploring. I found Jesus in Bali. In London. Morocco. Maybe not by name, but in spirit. In love. In presence. He was everywhere. I realized I don't need a church to feel God. I need stillness. I need truth. I need *intention*. That's where manifestation is born. From a heart aligned with gratitude, not a voice begging from fear.

Do you want to live your life as a prayer of gratitude or a prayer of worry? The choice is yours.

So many Christians try to "save" me now. But they don't realize I never left Jesus. I just left *them,* and their small-minded, judgmental ways. I left their version of Jesus. Their limitations. Their box. Not my faith. It's impossible to rewire your mind while clinging to a script someone else wrote for you.

Here's where science meets spirit:

When your beliefs are challenged, your brain reacts. The amygdala fires. Fight or flight kicks in. Your ego builds a wall. It's called the "totalitarian ego." It exists to protect the version of you you've always known. But transformation requires *surrender*. It requires questioning. And yes, it requires a little ego death. That's where the miracle happens. That's where the brain rewires. That's where you stop living from your past and start creating from your future. That's *neuroplasticity*.

You weren't born with your beliefs. You inherited them. Just like trauma. Just like behavior. You can choose to interrupt the pattern at any time, rewire your brain, raise your frequency, and manifest a whole new reality. *But only if you get honest.* Only if you stop outsourcing your faith, and start *embodying* it.

Heaven and hell aren't just places, they're frequencies. They live in your thoughts, your reactions, your choices. Every moment you choose resentment, fear, scarcity, you step towards hell. Every time you choose grace, forgiveness, gratitude, you step into heaven. You are the creator of your inner world. You always have been. That's what Jesus meant when He said, "The kingdom of heaven is within you." It is yours to create.

He was responding to the Pharisees, who were asking when the Kingdom of God would arrive. They expected something external, something political or powerful they could point to. Jesus shifted their understanding. He wasn't talking about a place to be seen or a throne to be built. He was revealing a deeper truth: ***the Kingdom starts within.***

That changed everything for me. I stopped waiting on something outside of me to bring peace. Heaven and hell aren't just destinations. They are often the emotional and spiritual states we create through our reactions, choices, and mindset.

When it comes to manifestation, that truth is everything. You can't manifest from a place of fear, doubt, or scarcity. You will keep living the same internal chaos. That's the cycle many of us call hell. However, when you begin to nurture peace, gratitude, and love from the inside out, you raise your frequency and create space for abundance to flow. The Kingdom within is real. It's not about perfection. It's about alignment. *It's available right here, right now.* Which is why creating your own meditation altar or sacred space, as we've discussed in this module, is so crucial. It is truly your access point to presence anytime you need it.

I didn't abandon my faith, I reclaimed it. I didn't lose Jesus, I found Him again, in stillness, in travel, in culture, in heartbreak, in healing, in rewiring my mind, in creating my life on purpose. I've come to believe all religions, at their core, are saying the same thing: Return to love. Return to truth. Return to yourself.

You don't need to be perfect to manifest miracles. You need to be *honest*. You need to stop performing, stop hiding, and start healing. You need to wake up and save yourself. You don't need a preacher, you need *presence*.

And baby, if that's what it means to be "a born-again Christian," then yes, I've *risen*. But I don't think that's what Good ole Brother Bill meant to manifest for me! Hey, sometimes I do listen.

Journal Entry

Embrace The Gift Of Today

This exercise invites you to deeply connect with the present moment by imagining the wisdom and perspective of your future self.

What You'll Need: A quiet space for reflection, a journal, a pen, and perhaps a timer set to 10 or 15 minutes, if that's helpful.

The Visualization Phase: Begin by closing your eyes and imagining yourself at 100 years old. Your life has been a beautiful, fulfilling journey filled with love, joy, and growth. Each day, you wake up with the understanding that it might be your last, and your heart, though full, is gently worn from years of living. Sit here a while. Allow yourself to feel the gratitude and joy that come with knowing you have lived a life rich in experiences. If tears come, let them flow as an expression of the love and appreciation you have for your journey.

The Gratitude Phase: Now, imagine a genie appears before you, offering you an extraordinary opportunity. The genie offers for you to return to this very moment you are reading this book today, and relive your life from here. With a heart full of excitement and gratitude, you eagerly say, "Yes! Let me do it all over again!"

The Manifestation Phase: Open your eyes and write about the emotions and thoughts that arise from this experience. How does the perspective of your 100- year-old self influence the way you see your life today? What small or big changes do you feel inspired to make? What would you do differently with this newfound opportunity to live again?

Reflect on how you can bring this deep sense of appreciation and purpose into your daily life. Commit to a few actions or mindset shifts that align with this renewed perspective.

The Renewal Phase: Revisit this exercise regularly to remind yourself of the gift that today is. Let it inspire you to live fully, with gratitude and intention, every day.

MANIFESTED

Module 3

Deepening Your Practice

3.1 Building a Strong Manifestation Foundation

Building a robust foundation is the cornerstone of successful manifestation.

The previous module focused on creating a sacred space for your manifestation work, while this module focuses on deepening your practice within that space. Here you'll find essential elements that form the bedrock of your manifestation practice. Let's dive in!

Identifying Personal Values

Identifying personal values is a crucial step in building a strong foundation for various aspects of life, including manifestation. Personal values are the core principles and beliefs that guide your decisions, actions, and overall life direction. Here's a step-by-step guide to help you identify your values:

1. Self-Reflection:

- Take time for introspection. Find a quiet space where you can reflect without distractions.

- Consider your past experiences, achievements, and moments of fulfillment. What values were present in those moments?

2. Examine Your Priorities:

- Look at your current priorities in life. What activities and relationships matter most to you?

- Identify the aspects of your life that bring you the most satisfaction and joy.

3. List Core Values:

- Begin by listing a wide range of values that resonate with you. Common values include integrity, honesty, compassion, family, creativity, growth, and many more. Be sincere here. Get honest with yourself and own what you *truly* value!

4. Prioritize Your Values:

- Once you have a list, prioritize your values in terms of importance. This helps you understand which values hold greater significance in your life.

5. Reflect on Decision-Making:

- Think about past decisions, both significant and minor. What values influenced those decisions?

- Consider situations where you felt conflicted or uncertain, and reflect on the values that might have been in conflict.

6. Align with Your Goals:

- Evaluate your current goals and aspirations. Do they align with your identified values?

- Ensure that your goals are in harmony with your core values to create a more meaningful and purposeful life.

- Staying stuck in a place not conducive to your core values will prolong your desires from manifesting.

7. Seek Feedback:

- Ask friends, family, or colleagues about the values they see in you.

- Sometimes, others can provide valuable insights that you may not have considered. Don't get stuck on this feedback, just *observe it.*

8. Refine and Revisit:

- Your values may evolve over time. Periodically revisit and refine your list as you grow and experience new aspects of life.

- Be open to reassessing your values based on changing circumstances and personal growth.

9. Create a Personal Values Statement:

- Consolidate your identified values into a personal values statement. This concise statement can serve as a guide for your decisions and actions.

10. Live in Alignment:

- Once you've identified your values, strive to live in alignment with them. This consistency will contribute to a sense of authenticity.

By engaging in this process, you'll gain clarity on what truly does and doesn't matter to you. Now, the inspired action is in your court. *What will you do?*

Establishing a Strong Belief System

By now you understand that manifestation, at its core, hinges on belief. Your conviction in your ability to achieve your desires fuels the Law of Attraction and attracts opportunities that align with your goals. But how do you build a strong belief system that unshakeably supports your manifestation journey? **Here are some key steps:**

1. Identify Limiting Beliefs:

- The first step is self-awareness. Acknowledge any negative thoughts or beliefs that might hinder your progress. These could be self-doubts like "I'm not worthy" or limiting beliefs like "Success is only for the lucky few."

2. Reframe and Challenge:

- Don't let limiting beliefs hold you back. Challenge them with evidence and positive affirmations. Replace "I'm not good enough" with "I am capable and deserving of achieving my goals."

3. Focus on Your Strengths:

- Shift your focus from limitations to your strengths and past successes. Remind yourself of times you overcame challenges and achieved your goals. This builds confidence and reinforces your belief in your abilities.

4. Surround Yourself with Positivity:

- Negativity breeds doubt. Surround yourself with positive influences and supportive individuals who believe in you and your dreams. Their encouragement and faith can significantly boost your belief system. You are a product of the five people you surround yourself with the most. So, choose wisely!

5. Visualize Success:

- Visualization is a powerful tool for building belief. Regularly spend time visualizing yourself achieving your goals, experiencing the associated emotions, and feeling the confidence of success.

6. Take Inspired Action:

- Belief without action is stagnant. Take consistent, inspired action toward your goals. Each step forward proves your ability and reinforces your belief in your potential.

7. Celebrate Victories:

- Acknowledge and celebrate your achievements, no matter how small. Recognizing your progress reinforces your belief in your ability to succeed and motivates you to keep moving forward.

8. Seek Inspiration:

- Surround yourself with stories of successful individuals who overcame challenges and achieved their dreams. Their journeys can serve as powerful reminders that anything is possible.

9. Be Patient and Trust the Process:

- Building a strong belief system takes time and dedication. Don't get discouraged by setbacks. Trust the process, stay focused on your goals, and never lose sight of your dreams.

Developing Resilience in the Face of Challenges

It's crucial to recognize that growth plays a pivotal role in our journey towards manifesting our desires effectively.

Just as a baby undergoes an incubation period before birth, personal growth also requires time, nurturing, and development. It's akin to planting seeds and observing their journey from sprouting to fruition. When we plant a seed, we don't simply stand and wait for it to grow tall. We understand that with the minerals provided by the universe in the soil, along with sunlight and rain, the seed will be taken care of. This basic principle is something we learn in school, yet we sometimes forget that humans follow a similar pattern of growth. Just like with plants and other living things, the universal elements are already there f or us.

Unlike plants that immediately grow upwards, humans need to establish roots first; our seeds grow downward, and then they spread wide. Only after laying down strong foundations can we begin to grow upward. However, this growth process isn't instantaneous. It requires time, patience, and even growing pains. Much like tending to a garden, if our foundations (roots) are not nurtured, our growth suffers.

Our growth is intricately linked to our environment. Just as plants thrive in favorable weather conditions and struggle in harsh seasons, humans also grow according to the conditions around us. If we find ourselves in a supportive and nurturing environment, our growth is likely to be healthy and abundant.

However, if our surroundings are challenging or detrimental, our growth may be stunted or conditional. Therefore, it's crucial to cultivate an environment and mindset that fosters growth and provides the necessary support for our journey of self-improvement and personal development. Just like with the alligator from Module 1.

3.2 Identifying and Overcoming Limiting Beliefs

Our deepest desires can remain elusive if we're unknowingly chained by limiting beliefs. These are negative thoughts or assumptions about ourselves, our capabilities, or the world that hold us back and hinder our manifestation journey.

Recognizing Common Limited Beliefs

Here are some of the most common limiting beliefs to be aware of:

About Yourself:

- **Self-worth:** "I'm not good enough", "I don't deserve success","I'm not capable."

- **Competence:** "I don't have the skills", "I'm not smart enough", "I'll never learn this."

- **Appearance:** "I'm not attractive enough", "I don't fit in", "People won't accept me."

About Your Goals:

- "This is impossible", "It's too difficult", "It's too late for me."

- Only lucky people achieve this", "Success is reserved for others", "It's not meant to be for me."

- "What if I fail?", "I can't handle rejection", "It's not worth the risk."

About the World:

- "The world is a dangerous place", "People can't be trusted", "It's not safe to take risks."

- "There's not enough opportunity", "The system is rigged against me", "It's impossible to get ahead."

- "Change is scary", "Everything is uncertain", "It's better to stay in my comfort zone."

Remember:

- These are just a few examples. Everyone has different limiting beliefs based on their unique experiences and perspectives.

- Recognizing these beliefs is half the battle. Once you identify them, you can begin to challenge them and replace them with empowering thoughts.

- Don't judge yourself! Limiting beliefs are normal, and everyone has them. What matters is recognizing them and choosing to move beyond them.

Tips for Recognizing Your Limiting Beliefs:

- **Pay attention to your self-talk:** What are the negative thoughts that frequently pop into your head?

- **Identify recurring patterns:** Are there specific areas where you tend to doubt yourself or feel limited?

- **Notice your emotional triggers:** What situations or challenges tend to activate your limiting beliefs?

- **Journaling:** Write down your thoughts and feelings related to any current goals and challenges.

Now assess. What patterns of belief do you notice? How might you begin to shift or reframe them?

Strategies for Transforming Limiting Beliefs

Transforming limiting beliefs takes a layered approach. Here are some effective strategies you can use:

1. Awareness and Acceptance:

- **Self-reflection:** Begin by recognizing your limiting beliefs through introspection, journaling, and observing your emotional triggers.

- **Acceptance:** Accept them as thoughts, *not truths*, and acknowledge that they don't define you.

2. Challenge and Reframe:

- **Question the evidence:** Ask yourself, "Is this belief true?" Challenge it with facts, experiences, and examples of the opposite.

- **Logical refutation:** Use logic to dismantle the belief. For example, instead of "I'm not good enough," remind yourself of your past successes and strengths. No room for a pity party if you want to manifest good things into your life!

- **Positive reframing:** Replace negative thoughts with empowering affirmations. Instead of "I can't do it," say, "I can learn and grow to achieve my goals."

3. Visualization and Affirmations:

- **Visualization:** Spend time vividly imagining yourself confidently pursuing your goals and experiencing the joy of success. Feel the positive emotions associated with achieving your dreams.

- **Affirmations:** Regularly repeat positive statements that counter your limiting beliefs. Infuse them with conviction and visualize yourself embodying them.

4. Action and Experience:

- **Take small steps:** Break down your goals into smaller, achievable steps and take action towards them. Each success builds confidence and weakens limiting beliefs.

- **Celebrate progress:** Acknowledge and celebrate

your victories, no matter how small. This reinforces your belief in your abilities and motivates you to keep going.

- **Step outside your comfort zone:** Challenge yourself to try new things and face your fears head-on. This demonstrates your capability and builds resilience.

5. Supportive Environment:

- **Seek inspiration:** Surround yourself with supportive individuals who believe in you and your dreams. Their encouragement can counteract negativity.

- **Role models:** Find mentors or role models who have overcome similar challenges. Their stories can inspire you and demonstrate the possibility of achieving your goals.

- **Professional help:** If needed, consider seeking help from a therapist or counselor who can guide you through identifying and overcoming limiting beliefs in a safe and supportive space.

Remember:

- Transforming limiting beliefs is a journey, not a destination. Be patient with yourself and celebrate your progress, no matter how small.

- Embrace challenges as opportunities. Use them to learn, grow, and strengthen your belief in yourself.

THE EGO TRAP

Sure, thinking is a necessary tool to navigate the world, but for most people, about 80-90% of their thoughts are repetitive, useless, and often harmful. This kind of compulsive thinking is like an addiction. It feels stronger than you, and it gives a false sense of pleasure that inevitably turns into pain.

Why are we addicted to thinking? Because we've come to believe that our thoughts define us. We've constructed a mental image of ourselves (the ego) based on our conditioning. This ego only exists as long as we keep thinking. It's obsessed with the past (because without it, who are we?) and the future (where it hopes to find happiness or peace).

It views the present through the lens of the past or reduces it to a stepping stone to some future goal. The real key to liberation lies in the present moment, but you can't find it while you're trapped in your mind.

Remember, thinking is just one small aspect of consciousness. It can't exist without consciousness, but consciousness doesn't need thought to exist.

Shared on Brooke's Instagram page: The Power Behind Your Thoughts

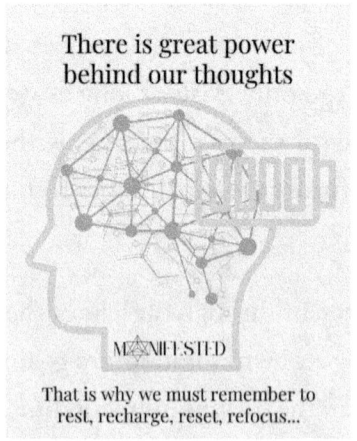

@get_connected_manifested

Go laugh in a place where you have cried.
Change your narrative.

Personal Story

Rewriting My Story, Rewiring My Beliefs

I knew if I truly wanted to make it out of the South, it would take more than a higher paycheck or a better job title. It would require unlearning. Stretching into the unfamiliar. Expanding my identity-not to erase where I came from-but to make room for what was never introduced to me.

In my hometown, college wasn't really discussed. Parents were proud just to see their kids graduate high school. Life afterward didn't shift much. Most stayed. Most lived within the same radius, driving the same streets, shopping the same stores, taking the same trips, maybe to a neighboring state if they were adventurous.

Worldviews weren't taught. History, barely. I thought my small town was the world. So, when I went off to a technical school, it felt major. I moved in with my high school best friend after getting kicked out of my stepfather's house for finally standing up to his narcissistic control. Then I married that same best friend. Because that's what you do. You settle down young, have babies, and try to make it work before you've even figured out who the hell you are.

I'm grateful for how it unfolded. I am grateful for my husband and my children, but I also see the patterns now-limited, inherited, and repeated.

My life began to crack open when I landed a job I thought was with a regular dentist, but he was far from regular. He was a world-renowned LVI-trained professional who offered cosmetic reconstructions worth tens of thousands of dollars. That role exposed me to a world of wealth, professionalism, and transformation I didn't know existed.

Still, despite my confidence and experience, I almost didn't get hired because of my accent. The dentist worried I'd scare off high-end clients. That I'd sound uneducated. So for the first few months, I wasn't allowed to answer phones. Instead, I pampered patients, baked cookies, refilled wine, made sure their VIP experience was perfect. I see now that I was cast into the role of Southern housewife because that's what my voice made them think I was best suited for. And honestly, I did it well.

Years later, after building real relationships with the team, the manager admitted this. She said she had planned to "train the accent out of me." (Sweet lady, thanks for trying!) But by then, I had proved myself. I had risen through the ranks. I learned just how powerful perception can be. I am not how others view my voice, *I am how I view me.*

To evolve, I didn't just have to get out of my town, I had to get out of the *mindset*. I had to stop shrinking. Stop toning down. Stop pretending that I was someone I wasn't, just to be accepted by people who didn't know me.

The shame I carried about my voice wasn't mine. It was projected. Then inherited. And it took deep work to shed it. I had spent over a decade in business rooms, board meetings, and strategy sessions where I was underestimated before I even completed my first sentence, not because of my ideas, but because of how I sounded.

For example, I think back to a hard memory like, the day when I was standing in front of a boardroom, ready to deliver a speech, confident and prepared, but before I fully began, a female executive walked out. I later learned she specifically left because of my accent. She assumed I wasn't worth listening to. Her peers confirmed it. That was the official feedback. *Wow. Sometimes I wonder how that woman turned out.*

That kind of judgment shaped me. I remember when I used to cringe at my voice on recordings, tried to neutralize my tone, speak slower, and use bigger words just to belong. Without realizing it, I sent out a frequency of unworthiness. I didn't hate myself, but I hated how I was perceived. That self-rejection blocked me from fully stepping into who I was.

Here's the truth: your vibration doesn't lie. You can speak affirmations all day long, but if deep down you don't *believe* you're enough, you are right...but only because you're misaligned.

My accent became a mirror. It held all my internal judgments. But when I chose to accept it, not just tolerate it, I noticed a shift. Not just in how I felt, but in what *I attracted*. Clients. Opportunities. Relationships. Everything responded to the frequency of wholeness instead of performance. This was alignment.

I used to think my accent made me less. Now, I see it as one of my greatest assets. It softens people, gives me an edge, and often causes others to underestimate me-which, honestly, works in my favor. It reminds me of where I come from and just how far I've come.

That's self-love. It's not blind praise or ego inflation. It's radical *acceptance*. It's standing in the mirror and saying: "You're allowed to be here. You're part of the story, too."

Manifestation isn't just about visualizing your dream life. It's becoming the version of you who feels worthy of it. Who already has it energetically. Who walks and speaks from alignment, not lack.

Sometimes, that journey starts by forgiving the parts of you that others made you ashamed of (i.e. your accent, your past, your fears.) All of it deserves love, because all of it is *you*.

My accent no longer makes me flinch. It reminds me I've walked through fire. That I've outgrown old beliefs. That I've evolved. My intelligence cannot be heard in the first word that rolls off my tongue, it is lived, embodied, and displayed through how I carry myself and my own self belief. I know that who I am is based on how I see and score myself, not how others do. Other's opinions are not true for me, they are true for them. The same applies to you!

PERSONAL STORY 143

```
                         3-4
          SCORE SHEET
                                yes.
     MISS DIXIE SWEETHEART PAGEANT
              TALENT
CONTESTANT #  17

EXECUTION .................. (40 POINTS MAXIMUM)  38

TECHNICAL DIFFICULTY ....... (20 POINTS MAXIMUM)  20

COSTUME .................... (20 POINTS MAXIMUM)  20

CONFIDENCE ................. (20 POINTS MAXIMUM)  20

TOTAL POINTS ............... (100 POINTS MAXIMUM) 98

COMMENTS  Cute costume -
          Very nice - Get her to
                          smile!!
Mothers & Daughters:
Thank you for participating in Miss Dixie Sweetheart
Pageant today. We hope you had an enjoyable time.   as
Remember ... The scores given today are the opinions  she
of one set of Judges.                                  sings
                                   Jewell Chancey
```

Check it out: 3 years old, singing, tap dancing and still not enough. "Get her to smile as she sings." 2 points off.

SCORE SHEET

MISS DIXIE SWEETHEART PAGEANT

PRO-AM MODELING

CONTESTANT # 17

POISE ....(20 POINTS MAXIMUM) 20

GROOMING ....(20 POINTS MAXIMUM) 20

ATTIRE ....(20 POINTS MAXIMUM) 20

PROJECTION ....(40 POINTS MAXIMUM) 40

TOTAL POINTS ....(100 POINTS MAXIMUM) _____

COMMENTS *projects wonderfully. Great smile!*

Mothers & Daughters:
Thank you for participating in Miss Dixie Sweetheart Pageant today. We hope you had an enjoyable time. Remember . . . The scores given today are the opinions of one set of Judges.

Jewell Chancey

Meanwhile, another judge gave me a perfect score and said my smile was beautiful. That's the thing about perfection, it depends who's holding the pen. And just like that, my worth was filtered through someone else's scorecard.

Journal Entry

The Idea Depository - Discovering Your Purpose

This practice helps you catch the seeds of your creative impulses and allow them to germinate into a purposeful vision to manifest.

What You'll Need:

A container (mason jar, box, bowl, etc) to serve as your "Idea Depository" Slips of paper/cards and a pen

The Deposit Phase:

1. Designate your chosen container as a sacred space to collect your imagination's expressions.

2. Whenever a random thought, desire, revelation, or creative burst arises, jot it down and deposit it into your container. These ideas can be unpolished or half-formed. Let them flow freely.

3. Release attachment after each deposit, allowing the ideas to gestate alongside the others.

The Synthesis Phase:

1. After accumulating deposits over weeks/months, spread them all out before you.

2. With a beginner's mind, look for patterns, themes, or connections between the ideas.

3. What creative sparks arise as you merge these data points of your consciousness? Where do you sense purpose emerging?

4. Cluster related ideas into potential pathways, projects, or undertakings you feel called to manifest.

The Manifestation Phase:

1. Choose 1-3 concept pathways that excite you and break them down into actionable goals.

2. Gather resources, make an action plan, and commit to birthing these aligned inspirations into reality.

3. Refresh your depository regularly, observing what continues blossoming from your depths,

ripe for manifestation.

This practice honors the totality of your creative mind, conscious and unconscious. By catching the sparks, synthesizing them into purposeful pathways, and taking action, you fluidly manifest your soul callings into lived reality.

MANIFESTED

MODULE 4

Living with Purpose and Intention

Now that we've set the stage for your practice, explored some foundational tools, and examined your belief system, it's time to truly begin embodying your manifestation journey. This module is all about living with purpose and intention, which is about more than just setting goals. This work is about showing up every day with clarity, focus, and a deep connection to who you are and what you truly want out of life. It's not always easy, but when you align your actions with your purpose, you start to feel a sense of flow and fulfillment that goes beyond simply checking things off a to-do list. This module will help you get clear on your personal purpose, set intentional goals that resonate with your values, and take practical steps toward manifesting the life you truly want. See how this all stacks? Let's dive in!

4.1 Defining Personal Purpose and Intentional Goals

Living with purpose starts by getting clear on what matters most to you. Too often, we get swept up in society's expectations, ticking boxes on someone else's checklist, whether it's getting the "right" job, earning enough money, or following a pre-set path. But here's the thing: your purpose is unique to *you*. It's that thing that makes you feel alive, aligned, and connected to something greater.

Defining Your Purpose

Think about the moments in your life when you felt most fulfilled or at peace. What were you doing? Who were you with? What values were you honoring in those moments? Your purpose doesn't have to be something grand or world-changing, it could be as simple as living a life of kindness, creativity, or connection. The key is that it's true to you.

Aligning Actions with Manifestation Goals

Once you've defined your purpose, it's time to set goals that are aligned with that purpose. Instead of just setting goals that sound impressive, focus on goals that genuinely resonate with your core values. For example, if your purpose is to inspire others, your manifestation goals might involve sharing your story through writing or teaching. The important thing is that your goals feel meaningful, not just "productive".

Ask yourself:

- Does this goal align with my purpose?
- Will achieving this goal bring me closer to the life I want to live?
- How does this goal make me *feel*? Excited, inspired, or obligated?

When you set goals from a place of purpose, you'll find that your actions start to feel more intentional, and life becomes less about "getting stuff done" and more about *living* in alignment with your higher self.

4.2 Practical Steps to Manifestation

Okay, now that you've tapped into your purpose and set some intentional goals, it's time to get practical. Manifestation is a beautiful blend of vision and action, it's about dreaming big, but also doing the work to bring those dreams into reality. This part of the journey requires you to set realistic goals, take inspired action, and be willing to adjust course as you go.

Setting Realistic and Achievable Goals

Let's be honest, sometimes we set goals that are so huge, they can feel overwhelming. While it's great to dream big, it's important to break those dreams down into manageable, bite-sized pieces. You don't have to move the mountain all at once. Focus on the next step in front of you.

For example, if your goal is to start a business, don't put pressure on yourself to have it all figured out in one go. Start by setting smaller, achievable goals like researching your market, building a website, or creating a business plan. Each small win adds up and keeps you moving forward.

Inspired Action and Progress Tracking

Taking action is where the magic happens. But not just any action, *inspired action*. This is when you take steps that feel aligned with your purpose and intention. These are the actions that don't feel forced or draining; they're the ones that excite you, even if they're small. Maybe it's reaching out to a mentor, signing up for a class, or starting that passion project you've been putting off. The key is to take action that feels like it's moving you closer to the life you envision.

Along the way, track your progress. Celebrate those small wins and use them as fuel to keep going. Keep a journal, mark milestones on a calendar, or use a vision board to remind yourself of how far you've come. Tracking your progress helps you stay motivated and gives you a tangible reminder that you're on the right path.

Addressing Doubts and Skepticism

Let's talk about the elephant in the room: *doubt*. No matter how clear your intentions are or how aligned your goals feel, there will be moments of self-doubt. You'll ask yourself, "Can I really do this?" or "What if I fail?". This is natural. Doubt isn't a sign that you're off track, *it's a sign that you're pushing beyond your comfort zone.*

The key is not to let doubt stop you. When those negative thoughts creep in, remind yourself why you started this journey in the first place. Remember your purpose, revisit your goals, and ask yourself, "What if I succeed?". Then *envision* that success. Really *feel* it, and play it out in your mind. Let that feeling replace any negative narrative.

One trick I use when doubt sneaks in is to focus on the smallest, next step I can take. Instead of getting overwhelmed by the big picture, I just do the next right thing; whether that's sending one email, writing one page, or taking 10 minutes to meditate and refocus.

Again, living with purpose and intention is about more than just setting goals, it's about creating a life that feels meaningful and aligned with who you truly are. It is all full circle.

By defining your personal purpose, setting achievable goals, and taking inspired action, you'll not only move closer to your dreams but also feel more connected to the journey along the way. Remember, manifestation isn't about perfection, it's about progress. Stay grounded, stay aligned, and trust that every step is bringing you closer to the life you're meant to live.

Sometimes the universe answers your call,
not with what you asked for, but with what
you're ready to receive.

Personal Story

I'll Choose London and Morocco Over Doubt Any Day

In 2022, I started using vision boards as a way to close out the year and set intentions and goals for the one ahead. It felt fun, inspiring, and gave me something to get excited about. But let's be real, I was still a total novice when it came to understanding what I was actually trying to call in. I did it because a social influencer made a pretty board and I wanted one, too.

Many of the items I put on that 2022 board ended up getting checked off, and that momentum had me fully committed to the "tradition" of "goal-setting" again in 2023. In my head, the things that came to life in 2022 could easily be chalked up to me following my roadmap and staying focused. I didn't credit much of it to "manifestation" at the time. Honestly, I still viewed manifestation as some woo-woo, mystical concept, fun to talk about, but probably not real. Silly me.

The truth is, I didn't know what I didn't know, and I genuinely love and hold space for that version of me. She was skeptical, yes, but also open to new things. She questioned it and still leaned in anyway. I couldn't ask for a better companion to be on this journey with than me.

At the end of 2023, I decided I was ready to manifest a trip to Morocco. I'd seen it on one of my yoga teacher's socials, and something about it just called me. I didn't know much about it, and hadn't traveled much outside the U.S., but I knew I wanted to go and was going to in 2024.

I printed out a picture of a map and glued it to my vision board. But here's the kicker: I printed out a photo of Europe because I thought that's where Morocco was. I know, "Bless my heart".

In my defense, I'd heard from friends that once you're "over there" it's easy to hop around Europe by train, ferry, or small plane. I just assumed Morocco was part of that general area. I even caught myself visualizing being able to squeeze in Paris or London while I was there. What I didn't realize at the time was that yes, a short ferry or small flight from Portugal can get you to Morocco, but you're crossing into an entirely different continent, not just another stop on the European sightseeing route. That realization came later and hit hard.

Still, the energy behind it was real. Every day, I looked at that board. I imagined the trip, the feeling of adventure, the expansion. I played it all out in my head. I fully believed I was calling it in. I was doing ALL the things.

By March 2024, life was piling up, and I realized I couldn't make the retreat scheduled for June 2024 happen that year. I let the organizer know I'd aim for the next one in 2025. Quietly, I felt disappointed, like maybe my vision board wasn't going to work. For a few days, I even resented it and let a wave of doubt creep in.

One day in May 2024, however, a free trip to London fell in my lap. Full airfare and hotel stay were completely covered. All I had to do was pay for food and experiences. I was elated. I Googled London to start planning, and as I zoomed out on the map, I thought, wait... *how far is Morocco from London?*

That's when it happened. You guys, I saw Morocco written in **_Africa._** I'd been visualizing a trip to Morocco, but the image I glued down was a map of Europe. The visuals in my head were full of European flare: the double-decker buses in London, the charm of high tea, and those classic city streets. Without even realizing it, I had manifested exactly what I asked for without words. I guess the saying "*ignorance is bliss*" applies here?

When the realization hit, I felt like the biggest idiot, and at the same time, unbelievably liberated and powerful. That was my full-circle, holy shit manifestation moment, and I cannot wait for you to experience yours.

This kind of thing happens to me all the time. Even when it doesn't look exactly like I imagined, it still shows up. The universe delivers in its own way, and if you're paying attention, it will show you. If you believe-

London was real. The vision was real. I walked through Buckingham Palace like royalty because my confidence game was strong, sister. That trip was my next level because I had *become* next level. Through confidence, self-belief, and inspired action I was a different version of me.

London, July 2024

At the end of 2024, I got clear. I printed out a picture of Moroccan spices and glued that image of Morocco on my new board. I set the intention again, this time with more awareness, more specificity, more growth, and less ego. Full faith.

In June 2025, I finally went and it was everything I dreamt of, and so much more. The group, the energy, the timing. It was all divine. I now understand why I wasn't meant to go in 2024, I was supposed to be there in 2025. The 2024 version of me wasn't ready; she was still in survival mode, still carrying armor, and still operating from ego, even while trying to manifest. This particular yoga teacher training was all about letting go, and I wasn't fully there in 2024. I would have still tried to hold the reins in and control.

The teacher training I did in Morocco was Yin-based. It was soft, powerful, and deeply feminine. It cracked me open in the best way. I won't unpack it all here, but it helped me shed the masculine energy I used to survive the past few years in the boardrooms. It invited me to trust, to surrender, and to heal through softness instead of control. *I've learned that control is just doubt masking itself as strength.*

I could tie this story into belief. Into vision boards. Into mindset, alignment, specificity, or surrender. Listen though, the real truth and picture to see here is this: it's not just one of those things, *it's all of them*, working together. Manifestation isn't a trick. It's not a one-time ritual you try on a Sunday afternoon with magazine clippings and candles. It's a way of living.

It's how you think. How you speak. How you recover when doubt creeps in and things don't go your way. It's trusting that the universe knows what is best, and hears your heart without words. It's how you handle delay and how you pivot when life throws you something unexpected. It's the faith you hold before the results show up. It's the vision you keep believing in, even when you accidentally glue the wrong continent to your board.

This journey reminded me that manifestation is not just about what you want. *It's about who you become while calling it in.* It's about living in alignment every day, not just hoping the universe reads your list. The belief is open, not closed. It isn't one sided, it is welcoming.

When you live this way, with vision, belief, presence, and patience, the life you create becomes the proof you so soulfully seek. No one can tell me manifestation doesn't work because I have now lived it, seen it with my own eyes, and felt it with my own heart. You can, too!

What was once painted on the vision board

Now brought to life. Morocco, June 2025

MASTER YOUR EMOTIONS

Emotions can be tough to deal with, especially when they're intense. They're like supercharged thoughts. They can easily pull you in and take you over. This creates a vicious circle; the thought feeds the emotion, and the emotion feeds the thought. All impacting your manifestation process.

At its core, every emotion comes from a deep, undifferentiated feeling of pain. This pain is a mix of fear, abandonment, and incompleteness. It's hard to put a name to it, but it's the pain of forgetting who you are in the moment.

The mind's job is to get rid of this pain, but all it can do is cover it up temporarily. The harder it tries, the worse the pain gets. It can never solve the problem because it's part of the problem.

But what about positive emotions, like love and joy? These aren't just emotions, they're also states of being. They come from your connection with your true self. You can catch glimpses of these states when your mind goes quiet, such as when you see something beautiful, push yourself physically, or find yourself in danger. You're able to access these states because you are deeply connected to yourself.

These states can't fully bloom until you break free from the dominance of your mind. But to do that, you need to be fully aware of your emotions first.

ILLUMINATE YOUR MIND

So, how do we break free from this struggle? It's all about *awareness.* When you lovingly shine the light of consciousness on the unconscious parts of your mind, they start to dissolve. The unease, tension, and discontent that come from judgment, resistance, or denial can't survive when you're fully aware of them. The dissolving of these emotional fluctuations takes practice, but ultimately creates greater balance.

To make this a habit, start checking in with yourself regularly. Ask questions like, "Am I at ease right now?" or "What's going on inside me?" Be as interested in your inner world as you are in the outer world. If you approach your inner world with more curiosity and less judgement, the outer world will naturally begin to fall into place in healthier ways.

When you ask these questions, don't jump to answer them right away. Take a moment to look inside yourself. Notice your thoughts and feelings. Pay attention to your body. Is there any tension anywhere, maybe in your arm or your chest? Get curious.

Once you realize there's some unease or background static, see if you're resisting the present moment in any way. There are countless ways people do this without realizing it. As you practice self-observation, you'll get better at spotting your unconscious patterns and learning how to shift them.

Storytelling

Another helpful tool is to ask other people to share their stories. Observe how they talk about hard moments. Witness the presence of emotions in their lives and how they choose to navigate them. By listening to other people's stories, you might just see yourself reflected in their journey. You might experience an 'Ah-ha' or 'me too!' moment. For this reason, I've decided to include a bonus personal story in this module. It touches specifically on the emotional alchemy of grief, but can be applied to any challenging emotion you may be experiencing. May it serve you, sister. You are not alone.

"I had been turning pain into power, grief into growth, and loss into love my entire life."

Personal Story

Emotional Alchemy - Grief, Energy, and the Frequency of Manifestation

Grief has a way of reshaping us. It's not just an emotion, it's a frequency. A dense, heavy energy. When my mother passed, it was the hardest thing I had ever experienced, but something positive happened in my life. When I say that, I don't mean that my mom's passing magically healed or fixed my life but it did illuminate something I had been practicing all along, without even knowing what to call it: ***emotional alchemy.*** I had been turning pain into power, grief into growth, and loss into love my entire life. What I thought was survival, was actually transformation.

Our emotions are energy. Energy is the language of the universe. It's what we emit, and what we attract back. This is the connection point between grief, healing, and manifestation. When we learn to sit with pain instead of suppressing it, when we allow it to move through us rather than harden us, we shift our frequency. We become more than what happened to us. We become vessels of intention, vibrating at the level of what we are ready to receive.

Love is the highest frequency of all. Not the kind sung about in pop songs or portrayed in romance novels, but the real thing, energetic love. Compassion. Presence. Understanding. Trust in something greater. If grief breaks us open, love is what rebuilds us from the inside out. Maybe that's what Jesus meant when He said, "God is love." Maybe He meant it literally. When dealing with love, we align with Source. We enter the highest manifestation field available to us. Most people don't realize this about manifestation: it's not about getting what you want, It's about becoming who you need to be in order to receive it. It's not about wishing, it's about wielding. You have to be an energetic match for what you desire, and that doesn't happen through bypassing your pain. It happens by transmuting it
.

The day of my mother's funeral, someone pulled me aside and asked, "Are you on something?" They weren't being rude. They were genuinely confused about how I could carry myself with grace in the middle of such loss. I didn't have an answer at the time. But now I know: *it was alchemy*. I wasn't bypassing the grief. I was present in it. I was choosing love over collapse. Presence over paralysis. Direction over destruction. I honored the weight of the grief in my body, allowing it to ground me, while also moving through the emotional tides inside. The storm was there internally, I just chose to use the energy in a different way. Flipping it into power didn't mean suppression. We are all just wired differently. That's what manifestation is at its core. It's not about pretending you're okay. It's about choosing what to do with the energy you have. Pain can bury you or birth something new. The energy is neutral, it's what you assign to it that gives it power. Every emotion carries a charge. Every experience presents a choice. And the most powerful manifestation doesn't happen when life is perfect. It happens when we rise from the ashes, anchored in love, grounded in truth, vibrating with clarity.

So, if you're grieving, know that your grief holds power. If you're angry, know that your anger can fuel clarity. If you're lost, know that you're in the exact place where a new direction can emerge. *You have to learn to observe and redirect it, instead of neglect and suppress it.*

Journal Entry

The Five Elements Within

Be a kid again! Don't skip over this exercise. Be willing to unlock your adult mind and see what happens.

Close your eyes and breathe deeply. Imagine your body is composed purely of the element of Fire. Every cell, every molecule, is condensed flames and scorching heat.

As Fire, you have an intense presence that immediately commands attention. Your very gaze and words are blasts of fiery breath. Take a few moments to write about this experience: How does it feel to be this radiant, all-consuming force of Fire? What happens when you try to write, but the paper and pencil burst into ash from your scorching touch? Is there a struggle to contain and control the blaze within?

Next, envision yourself transitioning into the flowing, shapeshifting form of Water. You are a cresting wave, a winding river, raindrops glistening on a spiderweb. Become one with Water's fluidity as you describe the sensations: How do your liquid limbs yearn to obey gravity's pull and merge into the downhill stream? Is it a challenge to maintain boundaries and structure in this form? Where does Water's path naturally want to meander?

Now feel your essence dispersing into the ethereal element of Air. You are a breeze caressing the meadow, a storm-stirred gale, the sacred breath of life itself. Give Air a voice as you write: How does it feel to be both the unseen force that animates all life, yet also a fleeting whisper that disappears into oblivion? Where does the Wind yearn to travel and what secrets does it carry? Is there a need for grounding?

Finally, root yourself into the dense, nourishing fabric of Earth. You are a mountain's granite permanence, the rich soil that births abundance, every grain of sand and volcanic rumble. Become the Earth as you describe: How does it feel to be the source that supports all living things, yet also so solidified and unchanging? Is there comfort or heaviness in Earth's planes and crevices? Where does her energy yearn to transform and flow?

After experiencing each of the Elements, call on aspects of all four to blend into the holistic harmony that is your true Self. You are all the forces ,both ethereal and solid, flowing and still, creative and nurturing.

In your journal, bring forth this integrated self-portrait. Explore your unique alchemy of Elements through words, images, colors, or any creative expression that arises. Embrace all aspects - temporal & timeless, expansive & grounded, intense & gentle. Describe how it feels to fully inhabit and radiate the wholeness of your nature.

Yes, for you adults that have forgotten what a crayon looks like or how to use it, do it!

By accepting all your "elements" exactly as they are, you alchemize into the masterpiece you were born to be.

MANIFESTED

MODULE 5

Affirmations and Intentions

In the process of manifestation, affirmations and intentions serve as tools for aligning your inner beliefs with your desired outcomes. When you combine affirmations with clear, powerful intentions, you create a direct line between your conscious desires and your subconscious mind, allowing you to manifest your goals with greater clarity and ease. In this module, we'll explore how to craft personalized affirmations, set meaningful intentions, and enhance the manifestation process by aligning your energy with your goals.

5.1 Creating Personalized Affirmations

Let's be real: life can sometimes chip away at our self-worth. We end up walking around with limiting beliefs we didn't even realize we had, like we're not smart enough, pretty enough, successful enough. But that's where affirmations come in, like a quiet, persistent friend reminding you of your worth every single day.

Crafting Affirmations for Success

To create effective affirmations, start by identifying the areas of your life where you want to see growth or change. Then, craft affirmations that are specific, present-tense, and positive. For example, instead of saying, "I want to be confident," reframe it to "I am confident and capable in everything I do." This subtle shift turns your affirmation into a statement of fact, reinforcing the belief that what you desire is already true.

Tips for crafting powerful affirmations:

Make it Personal: Don't be afraid to get specific. What do you need to hear? If you've struggled with self-doubt, affirm, "I am confident in my abilities, and I trust the path I am on." Make it something that hits home for you.

Speak in the Present Tense: This is key. It's about telling your mind that you're already living the life you want. Instead of "I want to be healthier," say, "I am thriving in my body, mind, and spirit." It's a subtle but powerful shift.

Keep it Positive: Focus on what you do want, not what you don't. Affirmations should make you feel good. So instead of "I don't want to be broke," say, "I attract abundance and financial ease."

The Psychology Behind Affirmations and Beliefs

Affirmations work because they help to reprogram your subconscious mind. Our minds are often filled with limiting beliefs that hold us back, many of which are deeply ingrained from childhood or past experiences. Affirmations help to overwrite those limiting beliefs by introducing new, empowering thoughts.

Through repetition, your brain starts to accept these positive statements as truth, making it easier to act in alignment with your goals.

Research has shown that positive affirmations can reduce stress, boost confidence, and improve mental well-being. By consciously repeating affirmations, you're training your mind to focus on possibilities rather than limitations.

Daily Affirmation Practices

Life gets busy, and it's easy to forget those affirmations you scribbled down. But here's the thing: affirmations work best with repetition. They need to be part of your daily rhythm.

Morning Ritual: When you wake up, before you grab your phone, start your day by repeating your affirmations. Stand in front of the mirror if you can, and say them with conviction. Look yourself in the eye and remind yourself of who you really are.

Affirmation Audios: One trick I love is listening to affirmations while doing mundane tasks. Whether I'm driving, cleaning, or walking the dog, I pop on a playlist of affirmations. It's such an easy way to reinforce them without needing extra time in your day.

Meditation: Combine your affirmations with a meditation practice as we discussed in the meditation module. As you close your eyes and breathe, repeat your affirmations in your mind. Let them wash over you, and really feel them resonate in your body. It's a beautiful way to set the tone for your day.

5.2 Setting Powerful Intentions

While affirmations work on reprogramming your subconscious mind, intentions give your life direction. They are the clear, focused desires that guide your actions and set the tone for what you want to attract into your life.

Defining Intentions vs. Goals

There's a subtle but important difference between intentions and goals. Goals are specific, measurable outcomes, things you want to achieve, like running a marathon or earning a certain amount of money. Intentions, on the other hand, are about the energy behind those goals. They are less about the outcome and more about the journey. For example, if your goal is to start a business, your intention might be "to create something meaningful that serves others."

Intentions guide your energy and actions without the attachment to a specific outcome. They create a space for flow, allowing the universe to respond in unexpected ways. Goals can be part of your intentions, but intentions create a deeper connection to your purpose.

Aligning Intentions with Core Values

The most powerful intentions are those that are rooted in your core values. What do you truly care about? What do you want your life to reflect?

Before setting any intention, ask yourself:

- What do I value most in life – freedom, love, growth, creativity?

- How do I want to feel every day, even when things aren't perfect?

- How do I want to show up in my relationships, my work, and my personal growth?

- Perhaps, return to some of the core values you wrote down during our work together in Module 3.

For me, I've always valued freedom: freedom from debt, freedom to travel, freedom to be present with my kids. So, my intentions are often around creating a life that reflects that. When your intentions are aligned with your values, they become effortless because they're coming from your heart.

BREAK FREE FROM THE MIND TRAP

THE TRUE GIFT OF AFFIRMATIONS & INTENTIONS

When we're caught up in our never-ending stream of thoughts, we lose touch with our inner calm, the very essence of spirit. This mental noise not only causes suffering, but also creates a false sense of self; a mind-made version of ourselves that's often full of fear and struggle.

When we identify solely with our minds, we build a wall of ideas, judgments, and definitions that prevent genuine connection. It separates us from ourselves, each other, nature, and even the divine. This wall of thought is what creates the illusion that we're all separate beings, instead of remembering the truth that we're all interconnected. We might believe in this concept of oneness, but it's only when we experience it firsthand that it becomes truly liberating.

To me, one of the most groundbreaking songs by *Whitney Houston, "The Greatest Love of All"*, eloquently serenades us to love ourselves more than anything. But, how can we work to achieve that type of self-love when we allow our minds to constantly work against us, not *for* us?

Our minds are incredibly powerful tools. But, just like any tool, they can be misused. I've found that thinking has become an imbalance in our lives, much like a disease. Just as cells dividing uncontrollably can lead to illness, our minds, when left unmanaged, can cause havoc.

Most of us don't actually use our minds; our minds use us. It's a common misconception that we are our minds. We're not. We're so much more than that. And yet, we've become slaves to our own thoughts. When we're not conscious of our thoughts, we become possessed by them, mistaking the mind for who we truly are in essence.

This is why affirmations and intentions, as discussed in this module, are so vitally important to the manifestation process. Affirmations and intentions act as powerful anchors to focus and calm the mind. They actively disrupt "monkey mind" patterns of overthinking or analysis in their tracks. You can't repeat an affirmation and be stuck in a mental loop at the same time. It's like trying to love and hate at the same time, it just doesn't work.

Affirmations help us to distance ourselves from identifying with the mind, and instead support us in harnessing the power of the mind to align with that which we *do* want to identify with-our positive manifestations!

Here's the good news:

When we recognize that we are not defined by our thoughts, we can start observing them from a different state of awareness. This is the beginning of true freedom. We uncover an expansive realm of intelligence that transcends thinking and realize that the mind is only a fraction of that. Beauty, love, joy, and inner peace all stem from a realm beyond the mind. This is where awakening begins.

A new beginning is wasted if you bring your old habits with you.

Personal Story

Money, Honey and the Affirmation of Enough

Scarcity is more than a lack of resources, it's a mindset. A frequency. A lens through which many people in the South have been conditioned to see the world. We were raised to believe that there's only so much to go around, so you better get yours before someone else does. That mindset doesn't just limit your wallet, it limits your worth, your relationships, your possibilities.

We somehow created an entire class of people driven by this scarcity. A class that believes they have to buy, buy, buy in order to feel something. To identify with something external. To prove that they belong or that they've made it. Instead of being taught to discover who they are from within, people were taught to perform who they are through what they own.

Scarcity makes you grasp. It keeps you in survival mode, and survival mode is *not* fertile ground for growth or manifestation. In fact, the more you cling, the more you repel. Scarcity attracts more scarcity, just like fear attracts more fear.

To shift into abundance, you have to dis-identify with the external things you want and take your process inward. You have to believe that what you desire is already yours, not because you faked it with a vision board, but because you truly feel aligned with it. That's the work. That's where neuroplasticity comes in. Your brain has to be rewired. Your beliefs, repeated and reinforced long enough, become your reality.

This is why people get stuck. To rewire your brain, you have to first get honest about the wiring you already have. The lies you've believed. The stories you've inherited. And I get it, that's not easy in a culture where questioning those stories is seen as rebellion rather than reflection.

I remember working for a luxury dental practice where I was exposed to real wealth for the first time. I had never been around people who didn't blink at $80,000 dental treatments. I was in awe and I was also deeply insecure. I was reminded of how different I was. How I sounded. How I dressed. How I carried the South with me in every vowel, even when my thoughts were sharp and my instincts on point.

Eventually, I came to understand this: my accent wasn't the problem. My energy was. I carried insecurity, and the world reflected that back. I carried shame, and the world confirmed it. But once I started accepting myself, fully, accent and all, I began to shift my frequency. I stopped attracting people who made me feel small and started aligning with people who saw me clearly, now looking back, it was the same people the only difference was me.

Self-love isn't fluff. It's frequency. When you begin to truly love who you are, as you are, you stop seeking permission to be. You move differently. You attract differently. You create differently.

This is the missing piece in most manifestation conversations. You can't manifest abundance from a place of self-hate. You can't manifest love while rejecting your own reflection. You can't align with a better life while vibrating at the level of your past.

This is why when I think of applying affirmations to my own life, I often think of my affirmation work with money. In moments when I start to feel scarcity creep in, I don't chant, "I love money" 100 times a day. Instead, I use the simple affirmations, such as, "I am" or "So Hum," which literally translates to "I am that." Every time I think, write, chant or speak these affirmations, I am literally affirming to the Universe that *I am* money. *I am* abundance. *I am* security. These affirmations help me remember that I am not separate from abundance, but that abundance is literally within me.

Raising your frequency means integrating all parts of yourself. It means saying: "This is who I am. Unapologetically. I may still be growing, but I no longer need to perform worthiness." That's the kind of abundance the South isn't ready for yet. They aren't done with their victim mentality and self-inflicted pain. Where everything happens "to them", not for them.

If you're reading this book, you are inherently ready to remember your own worthiness. So, as you continue on your manifestation journey, play with the power of affirmations and have fun stepping into greater levels of abundance along the way!

Journal Entry

Excavating Answers - Blackout Poetry For Manifestation

Our conscious mind often struggles to find solutions, while our subconscious holds deep wells of wisdom. This exercise uses blackout poetry to tap into your unconscious truth.

What You'll Need:

- A printed page from a meaningful source (literature, spiritual text, famous speech(i.e. The Declaration of Independence or Shakespeare)

- Highlighter

- Thick black marker

- Your manifestation journal

The Exploration:

1. In your journal, write out a challenge, dream, or question you'd like to find a new perspective on.

2. Below it, freely list 5-7 additional questions or thoughts inspired by your main focus.

3. Next, take your chosen printed page. Read it over with an open mind.

4. Using your highlighter, highlight any words or short phrases that unexpectedly grab your attention or feel resonant.

5. Now read through the full text again. This time, blackout (mark over) every other word except the ones you circled.

6. The remaining "islands" of words will form an organic, subconscious-generated poem.

7. Read your blackout creation out loud and write it down in your journal.

The Reflection:

- What truth, insight, or recurring theme seems to emerge from this raw poem?

- Is there wisdom here your conscious mind overlooks? New ways of seeing your challenge?

- Sit with the poem and any feelings, images, or ideas it provokes within you.

This practice helps you bypass your conscious filters and delve into unseen spaces for fresh manifestation answers. By letting go of control and looking for new connections, you engage the vast intuitive knowledge your subconscious contains.

Repeat this blackout reading as inspiration strikes. See what deeper truths await discovery when you creatively excavate the spaces between the lines.

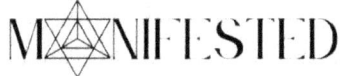

MODULE 6

Integration and Embodiment

6.1 Becoming a Conscious Creator

This final module is all about integrating everything you've learned throughout this journey. It's not just about manifesting one dream or goal, it's about stepping into the role of a conscious creator in your life. Manifestation isn't a one-time event; it's a lifestyle, a way of living with intention, abundance, and deep alignment. By the end of this chapter, you'll understand that manifesting your dreams is just the beginning. The real magic happens when you embody these principles every day and create a life that reflects your true essence.

What Does it Mean to be a Conscious Creator?

Becoming a conscious creator means realizing that you are always creating whether you're aware of it or not. Every thought, every intention, every action is shaping the life you're living. But here's the beautiful part: when you become conscious of this process, you get to choose what you're creating. You're no longer living on autopilot or reacting to life; you're actively shaping your reality with purpose.

Being a conscious creator means living intentionally. It's about taking ownership of your energy and aligning it with the life you truly want. It means understanding that life isn't happening to you, it's happening *through* you.

You're not waiting for things to change, you're the one creating the change. You've already done the work to shift your mindset, set your intentions, and take inspired action. Now, it's about fully stepping into this power and understanding that you are the creator of your reality-every single day.

6.2 Trusting the Process: Embracing the Unknown

Here's the part of manifestation that doesn't always get talked about: patience and trust. Sometimes, you do all the "right" things, set the intention, take inspired action, embody the energy, and yet, it feels like nothing's happening. This is where most people start to doubt themselves. But this is where the real growth happens.

The Power of Patience and Trust

Trusting the process means surrendering control and allowing the universe to work on your behalf. It means knowing that what you desire is already making its way to you, even if you can't see it yet. The truth is, manifestation isn't always instant. Sometimes, it takes time for the pieces to align in ways we can't predict.

During these moments, remind yourself that you're planting seeds. Just because you don't see the flower yet doesn't mean it's not growing. Keep tending to your desires with love, patience, and trust. The universe is always working behind the scenes, often in ways that are far greater than you could ever imagine.

Embrace the unknown with curiosity, rather than fear. Know that even the detours and delays are part of the journey, guiding you toward something even better than you planned.

6.3 The Infinite Journey: Manifesting as a Lifelong Practice

Manifestation isn't something you check off a list, it's an ongoing practice. As you grow and evolve, your desires will change. What you manifest today may shift tomorrow, and that's part of the beauty of this journey. Being a conscious creator means being open to continuous growth, knowing that there's always something new to learn, experience, and embody.

As you continue on this path, keep asking yourself:

- How can I deepen my alignment with my purpose?

- What new desires are unfolding within me?

- How can I expand my vision of what's possible for my life?

Remember, the universe is limitless, and so are you. There's no cap on what you can create. The more you open yourself to new possibilities, the more the universe will deliver.

The Journey of Becoming

By now, you've probably realized that manifestation is as much about who you become in the process as it is about achieving a specific goal. This journey isn't just about getting things, it's about becoming the person who is aligned with their highest truth, their deepest desires, and their fullest potential.

You've learned how to set intentions, how to use affirmations, how to take inspired action. You've practiced patience, trust, and surrender. But the real transformation is in who you've become along the way; a conscious creator, someone who knows their power and lives with purpose and alignment. Someone who believes their energy is sacred.

Take a moment to reflect on how far you've come. Maybe you're still on the path to manifesting your biggest dreams, and that's okay. The journey itself is where the magic is. The growth, the challenges, the moments of doubt-all of it has shaped you into the powerful creator you are today.

You Are The Creator

You are the creator of your life. You always have been, and you always will be. Everything you've learned here is simply a reminder of the power that's always been INSIDE of YOU.

There's no need to rush or force anything. The universe is always responding to your energy, and as you align more with your true self, your life will reflect that alignment. Trust the timing, trust the journey, and trust yourself.

You are capable of creating anything you desire, whether it's love, abundance, freedom, or inner peace. The tools are in your hands, and the power is within you. Now, it's up to you to live as the conscious creator you are.

Embrace the unknown. Trust your process. And remember: you've already got everything you need to create the life of your dreams.

You're not failing to manifest.
You're forgetting how to receive.

Personal Story

The Missing Step: Becoming a Skilled Receiver

Learning how to manifest is only one part of the equation when it comes to stepping into your desires. You must also practice receiving.

Many people focus on the creation process: visualizing, scripting, setting intentions, aligning energy. These are powerful tools. However, if you don't know how to receive what you've called in, you may unintentionally block or reject the very thing you worked so hard to attract.

Plenty of podcasters, influencers, and manifestation coaches speak about manifesting. Few emphasize that it is a two-step process. They often guide you through visualizing, affirming, and aligning your energy, but leave out the most essential follow-through: learning how to receive.

Here is the truth:

Manifesting + Receiving = Actual Manifestation

Calling something in without learning how to hold it or believe in it is incomplete. The real result of your desires arriving comes not just from intention, but from your ability to allow and support the energy once it shows up.

This is where chakra work, energy clearing, potential therapy, and deep self-love become essential. These practices help you access the parts of yourself that often block your blessings.

For many of us raised in the South, where generational patterns and conditioning run deep, this part of the process becomes especially challenging. The work is not just about creating a new life. It is about becoming someone who believes she is allowed to live it.

Manifestation and receiving are not the same thing. They are two distinct steps in the process. Both must be practiced.

Manifestation is the art of calling something in. It involves visualizing it, aligning with it, believing in it, and doing the energetic and intentional work to bring it closer to your reality. This is something I have gotten very good at. I have manifested clients, homes, opportunities, and trips-big things. I know how to set intentions, shift energy, and stay focused. Despite that, I have also completely messed some things up. I have watched blessings slip through my fingers, not because the universe was not delivering, but because I was not ready to hold them. That realization stings, but it has become part of the truth I am learning to accept. Naming it has helped me grow. Healing cannot happen without that kind of honesty.

Many of us are skilled at manifesting yet unskilled at receiving. This is why manifestations stall or dissolve. They show up, but they do not stay.

There are moments when I do not understand what hijacks my ability to receive. Sometimes it feels like hormones, or stress, or old self-sabotaging patterns that I still have not fully healed. I can feel myself disrupting the very thing I worked so hard to bring in. On some days, my self-belief fades. I feel small, unworthy, or uncertain. There are times when I even question whether I asked for too much. I begin to fear what stepping into the next version of myself might require letting go of what is familiar, what is comfortable, or who I have always been. These thoughts, though often quiet and subtle, are powerful enough to push everything I invited right back out the door.

This is not because I lack belief in the manifestation process. I do believe in it. The issue lives somewhere deeper, in the quiet places where doubt and fear still linger. Old identities attempt to pull me backward, even as my spirit tries to move forward.

The most painful part is knowing that it is happening while it happens. I am human, though, and this is part of the process.

There are weeks when I feel aligned, calm, and clear. I do the work. I feel good. I stay consistent. Then the manifestation starts to appear, and something shifts. Doubt enters. My nervous system reacts. My mind spirals or my energy shuts down. I slip into old habits. What I manifested starts to fade, not because I failed, but because I had not strengthened my ability to receive. It's a humbling process, and truly takes work.

Another truth we must acknowledge is this: not all confidence is rooted in true self-worth. Many of us carry confidence that is actually ego in disguise. This version of confidence can take you far. It can help you get noticed, close the deal, lead the room, and even manifest things. However, the universe sees through it when no one else does.

Ego-based confidence can manifest. IT CANNOT RECEIVE.

Receiving requires something deeper, unshakable self-love, true self-belief, and the ability to remain grounded when nothing is performing. This is where many of us get stuck. Hormones shift. The body tightens. Emotions rise. Our confidence wavers. Without inner work, this is where everything unravels.

Self-acceptance is what allows expansion. **You must believe in your vision, yes, but you must also believe in yourself enough to hold it**. At your core, you must know you are worthy of what you desire.

Receiving is not passive. It is an active, intentional practice. It requires nervous system awareness, emotional maturity, and willingness to step outside of your comfort zone. Receiving demands a sense of safety in the abundance. It invites you to hold more, not run from it.

There are times when I rise above my spiral. I remind myself I am safe, I am ready, I am enough. There are also times when I do not. I sit in the pity. I let the old narrative win. The thing I called in slips away, not because I lacked desire, but because I lacked integration.

Being aware of these moments does not always make them easier. However, awareness gives me a starting point for redirection. It helps me interrupt the spiral sooner and return to alignment. I notice myself getting better and better at this overtime, so trust me, it is possible for you, too.

Most people will never see those parts. Not because I am ashamed, but because I created my Instagram space as a place of motivation. My page is not where I unravel every emotion. It is where I celebrate my progress, give thanks, and reflect on what I am building. I use it as a tool of vision, not avoidance. My losses are not ignored, but I do not center them. They refine me. They are not my identity.

I stay honest on my page. My voice, my views, my energy are real. However, I choose not to highlight the lows in that space. I use that space to remember how far I have come and to continue moving forward. It helps me focus on the version of myself I am becoming, not who I was.

If you ever find yourself scrolling through manifestation pages, wondering why your life doesn't feel like theirs, remember this: everyone is still struggling with something. Every manifestor you admire is still a human being. No one escapes the work.

Manifestation is not magic. It is energy, plus intention, plus action. Manifestation requires tools. It also requires responsibility. Without a strong foundation, nothing sticks.

You need intention. You need specificity. You need effort. You need belief. You need action. You need regulation. You need heart. Manifestation is not a spell. It is not a potion. It is not a quick fix. You will still stumble. You will still cry. You will still have to grow.

However, if you stay committed to the process, if you stay willing to receive, you will also rise in the most beautiful and extraordinary ways.

I do not have it all figured out. I am writing this in the middle of it. I have chosen to walk this path while healing, while unlearning, while rewriting.

I was raised in the South, where women were taught to shrink. I carry generations of beliefs that do not belong to me. Trying to spiritually evolve while carrying ancestral wounds is no small thing.

If you have ever blocked your blessing, you are not broken. If you have ever questioned your worthiness, you are not alone. If you have ever doubted your ability to receive, you are still worthy of receiving.

Manifestation is a mirror. Receiving is the reflection of your self-worth.

To close the loop and step into your fullest expression, you must be able to say:

I believe in this vision.

I believe in me.

I am ready to receive what is already mine.

Journal Entry

Discovering Your Primal Self

For this exercise, find a quiet space where you can sit comfortably on the floor. Take a few deep breaths to center yourself, then close your eyes.

Imagine that you are in the warm, safe confines of the womb before birth. Feel the gentle rocking and muffled sounds as you float in peaceful existence. When you're ready, visualize yourself being born into a lush, primal landscape unseen by human hands.

As a newborn, you are lovingly cared for not by human parents, but by the nurturing animals and provided sustenance by the abundant plants around you. No words are spoken, as you need no language in this Eden. You learn solely through instinct, observation and felt connection with all life surrounding you. In this state, you know nothing of societal constraints, religious dogmas or ingrained belief systems. You are one with the rhythms of nature, tuned into the profound intelligence of the Earth. Your only guides are the sun, moon, weather and seasons.

After several years of this wild, feral living, you discover signs of human civilization in the distance. Imagine leaving your primal home and venturing into a nearby city or village. For the first time, you encounter artifacts of culture: houses, roads, temples, markets full of people conversing in a language foreign to your ears.

As you absorb the dazzling sights, sounds and even smells of this new world of human construction, what feelings or sensations arise within you? Are you frightened, curious, repulsed or excited by it all? Note the shift in your state as you, a pure product of nature, bear witness to this expression of human mind. If you chose to learn the language spoken here and assimilate to some degree, what would be difficult or easy to adapt to? What cultural beliefs, norms or taboos would rub against your innate, primal knowing?

After this significant realization, write a stream-of-consciousness account of your journey; from existing in idyllic oneness in the womb of the Earth, to being abruptly immersed in society's artificial world. Where did you feel most vibrantly alive and expansive? What did you have to reject, resist or conform to in order to "fit in"? How much of your primal self did you have to sacrifice?

This imaginative exploration can shed light on aspects of yourself that may have been conditioned or blocked by cultural programming. Use the experience as a way to reawaken your core, essential nature and notice what beliefs or patterns no longer serve your highest self. The present moment is your gateway back to that raw, unbridled state of being.

MANIFESTED

MODULE 7

Bonus Module: Energy is Everything

Finding Balance Between Dominance and Submission

Although this module wasn't included in my original MANIFESTED retreat guide, I've decided to include it here in the book for a more in depth consideration for your practice. So far, *Waking Up in the South* has focused on the 'what' of manifestation, but the energy behind *how* you manifest is just as important. They say, "The way you do anything, is the way you do everything." I don't know if I totally agree with that, but I do think it is crucial to examine how you typically move through life energetically. As doing such will have a direct impact on your manifestation journey. This module presents a basic understanding of masculine and feminine energy. I hope it serves to spark self-reflection and further exploration on your path.

Let's begin!

Manifestation isn't just about positive thinking or detailed vision boards. It's about learning to work with your full energetic system, your drive and your surrender, your action and your stillness. It's about learning when to lead and when to let go. In other words, it's about finding the balance between **dominance and submission**, both within yourself, and in the way you relate to life.

This balance can be described in many ways. You may have heard it taught as **Yin and Yang**, **feminine and masculine**, **receptive and active**, **being and doing**, or even **softness and strength**. These are not gendered ideas, but archetypal energies that live in each of us.

No matter which language resonates most with you, the core teaching is the same:

True power comes from integration. Manifestation requires both energy and ease, both surrender and action.

Most people tend to operate from one predominant energy. Some push hard, hustle constantly, and try to control outcomes (dominant, masculine, Yang-driven energy). Others wait passively, meditate, and trust the universe to provide without taking action (submissive, feminine, Yin-driven energy). Manifestation doesn't thrive in extremes. It thrives in *balance.*

This module will walk you through how to recognize *your* predominant tendencies, identify where you may be out of balance, and learn how to consciously work with both sides to bring your desires into form, not just by thinking about them, but by **embodying them.**

Understanding the Energetic Spectrum

While everyone carries both dominant and submissive energies, most people unconsciously lead with one. Recognizing your patterns is the first step toward balance.

Dominant (Yang) Energy Traits

- Action-oriented
- Goal-driven
- Logical and analytical

- Structured and decisive

- Pushes forward and initiates

- Controls outcomes or environments

- Often struggles with rest, surrender, or trust

When overused: May lead to burnout, rigidity, control issues, anxiety, or over-identification with performance or results.

Submissive (Yin) Energy Traits

- Receptive and intuitive

- Emotionally attuned

- Creative and visionary

- Flowing and adaptable

- Trusts timing and universal support

- Processes internally before acting

- Often avoids structure, confrontation, or assertive action

When overused: May lead to stagnation, indecision, lack of boundaries, passivity, or spiritual bypassing.

Why Both Are Required for Manifestation

Yin / Submissive Energy

- Envisions the desire
- Feels the frequency
- Trusts the unfolding
- Allows inspired timing
- Nurtures the "why"

Yang / Dominant Energy

- Takes action
- Builds the container
- Sets clear direction
- Executes and moves forward
- Handles the "how"

If you've ever felt like your manifestation practices are either too passive or too forced, this may be why. Imbalance in your energetic approach can block the flow.

Too much Yang may lead to chasing without clarity or burnout from trying to force results.

Too much Yin may keep you dreaming endlessly without anchoring any of it into reality.

The goal is not to eliminate one or choose a side. It's to integrate them. Let your Yin inspire the vision and your Yang build the bridge.

Quick Self Check-In

Take a moment to reflect. Ask yourself:

- Do I tend to over-plan, overwork, or try to control outcomes?

- Do I often avoid structure, timelines, or decision-making in the name of flow?

- Do I take aligned action, or wait too long for a sign?

- Do I allow myself to rest and receive without guilt or fear?

Your answers will reveal your energetic patterns. The goal is not to judge them, but to meet them with awareness and curiosity. *Where are you being guided to find more balance?* To **embody** this awareness, try inviting just one new habit into your life, and observe its effects. For example, if you're someone who typically has dominant energy and is always pushing and attempting to control outcomes, you'll want to balance your life by infusing it with more submissive or feminine energy. This could look like delegating tasks at work instead of trying to do everything on your own. Or scheduling a self-care day at the end of your week instead of engaging in workaholism. On a relational level, it could also look like you learning how to allow others to invite you to spend time together instead of you always being the one to initiate plans.

If you are someone who typically engages with life in a more submissive way, you'll want to add more dominant energy to help balance you. This could look like creating a weekly schedule that includes a dedicated morning practice. This could look like writing a business plan instead of staying in the dreaming or visioning stages of a business idea. Relationally, it could look like you making the first move instead of waiting for someone to ask you out on a date.

The options are endless! It might feel awkward at times, but try to have fun and give yourself grace as you begin to flex these new energetic muscles.

Integration Is the Practice, and It Takes Practice.

As I've said many times throughout this book, manifestation is not magic, it's *alignment*. And alignment requires balance. You are not meant to live in constant dominance, control, and output. You are also not meant to stay passive, invisible, and endlessly waiting. You were designed to **co-create**, to both **lead** and **receive**.

The more you understand the rhythm between your inner Yin and Yang, the more easily you will be able to move from vision to reality.

This is not just a method. It is a way of being.

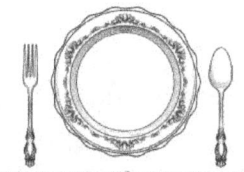

We were raised to serve supper
and silence. But some of us
grew hungry for more.

Personal Story

Reclaiming Our Feminine

There's a difference between leadership and control, but in the South, that line has been blurred for generations.

Like many Southern women, I spent years being charming, ambitious, and capable, yet still overlooked, underestimated, or expected to stay small. Not because I lacked power, but because I was taught to tuck it behind a smile.

That's where a lot of us get stuck, especially when it comes to manifesting. Manifestation doesn't happen in the energy of pretending. It can't move through performance. It flows through authenticity, alignment, and safety in your own skin.

Southern women have been told for generations to stay small. To be gentle. To be agreeable. To pour ourselves into appearances. To be submissive to men. That programming runs deep. I didn't see it clearly until I started traveling more.

Not just to other countries, but within the U.S.

I remember one of my early business trips to New York. I was walking through the city and noticed something that stopped me: the women looked different. Confident. Effortless. Some wore no makeup at all. Their hair was natural, undone, unbothered. But their energy? Fully owned. They didn't need a mask. They embodied their light.

But what struck me even more was this: *they didn't stare.*

Back home in the South, being a "pretty girl" always came with a cost. I was used to sideways looks, exclusion, and whispers. Judged before I ever opened my mouth. The stares didn't stop in adulthood. Walk into a restaurant in the South, and six sets of eyes will follow you to your table, not with admiration, but with insecurity. There's a certain pain in the way Southern women look at other women. A silent competition bred from years of being taught that our value comes from our appearance, our proximity to male approval, and how well our beauty stacks up against someone else's.

But in the North, it was different. Those women didn't flinch. They didn't compare. They didn't scan me for flaws or stare me down. They didn't even notice me. They were so grounded in their own bodies, confident on their own two feet. That kind of energy doesn't repel or compete, It just *is*. It made me feel, for the first time in a long time, like I didn't have to defend my presence. I didn't have to shrink to make someone else feel good or safe.

As I continued working up North and in the Midwest, I started noticing something else. Women up there don't take shit. They don't beg to be respected. They just are. As a result, their energy commands something. Men hold doors, pull out chairs, and meet them with a different kind of reverence. These women stand in their power but still embrace their feminine. There is balance. Grace. No need to perform or overdo. Meanwhile, down in the South, many of us are still fixing plates for our men, feeding their egos with their bellies, and taught that our worth lies in how well we serve.

Let me be clear: I'm not speaking for all women. These are simply my observations from my walk of life. Class plays a huge role, and there are always outliers. But the patterns I witnessed were enough to shift something in me.

The truth is, many of us didn't start out hardened. We became that way. We leaned fully into our yang energy, embracing the grind, the structure, the control. Not because we rejected our feminine nature, but because we believed that's what it took to rise above the limitations we were born into. It was how we took back control, not just from men, but over our lives. Over our direction, our choices, our voice. We took ownership of our income so we wouldn't have to rely on someone else, so we could have options. We know all too well that many women stay in unhealthy marriages or powerless situations simply because they can't afford to leave. No money. No safety net. No place to go. That realization woke something up in us and we built our own way out.

We wanted our voices, but we didn't realize it would cost us our softness. Over time, we calcified. We armored up. We got loud just to be heard in rooms that never really saw us. We gained power, but we lost ease. We survived, but we stopped flowing.

We lost our yin. Our softness. Our fluidity. Our ability to receive without gripping. We didn't just rise. We braced. Locked down. Shut off.

So, what do I mean when I say masculine and feminine energy?

We all carry both, regardless of gender. Masculine energy is the part of us that is structured, focused, driven, and protective. It's logical, assertive, and action-oriented. Think building, achieving, doing. Feminine energy, on the other hand, is intuitive, nurturing, creative, and receptive. It's about being, feeling, flowing, and allowing.

The goal isn't to choose one or suppress the other. It's to integrate both. When we're in balance, our masculine creates the container, and our feminine fills it with life. But when we live in survival mode, many of us, especially women, overcompensate by staying stuck in masculine energy. Because that's what has kept us safe.

We become hard because the world isn't soft. But now, our survival energy is draining us. Manifestation doesn't respond to burnout. It responds to alignment. And alignment means reconnecting to the parts of us that were never broken, just buried.

True power isn't always loud or forceful. Sometimes it is calm. Sometimes it is still. Sometimes it speaks without saying a word.

If you are ready to manifest a new chapter, a new life, or a new version of yourself, ***do not*** begin by doing more. Begin by remembering who you were before the world told you who to be. Come back to your center, to the version of you that trusts, receives, and creates with intention, not urgency.

That version, the one who is no longer overcompensating, is the version that magnetizes everything she desires. That is where the power is. That is where alignment begins. Remember: manifestation begins in the body. And it begins when we stop overcompensating and start *becoming*.

Resources as You Continue Your Journey

As we conclude our journey through the principles of manifestation together, I'd like to leave you with a suggestion for further exploration: delve into the world of chakras. If you haven't already ventured into understanding the chakra system, now is the time!

If you've never heard of the chakras before, it's important to know that according to yogic philosophy, they are energy centers that exist within the human body. These energy centers begin at the base of the spine and rise up to the crown of our head. Traditionally, yoga states that there are 7 of these core spiritual power centers in the body. However, science is now confirming that there are upwards of 12. When the chakras are aligned and properly functioning they can profoundly impact our health and wellbeing, as well as positive manifestations in our life.

Learning how the chakras function, from the foundational root to the enlightening crown, holds immense potential for insight on your personal journey. Adding chakra work to your manifestation practice will surely bring depth and greater embodiment; powerfully impacting your experience as a conscious creator.

For those eager to embark on this transformative path, I recommend diving into *"Eastern Body, Western Mind," by Anodea Judith.* This insightful book serves as a comprehensive guide to understanding and balancing your chakras. It is an approachable text to every reader, whether you are a total beginner or an advanced practitioner, and offers an array of both practical and spiritual support.

In addition to chakra work, I encourage you to explore *"The Power of Now," by Eckhart* Tolle. If you are ready for more in-depth insights regarding themes we've covered in this book, such as presence, limiting beliefs, and working with the mind, I can assure you, Eckhart's book will take your manifestation practice, and life, to a whole new level.

As you continue with your manifestation journey, pay attention to what other books or resources cross your path and inspire you. There are no coincidences!

Manifestation Is an Initiation

Throughout this book I've presented tangible skills and practices, as well as my uniquely personal lens on manifestation as a Southern woman. As you know, many people begin practicing manifestation because they want 'things'-new homes, jobs, relationships, or experiences. But as I've stated many times, manifestation is less about the objects you acquire and more about who you become in the process of aligning with them.

From a spiritual perspective, simply put, manifestation is an *initiation.* Initiation is the transformative process of meeting one's personal limits or thresholds, and *moving beyond them.* The result is often a shift in consciousness and an expansion of one's capacity for life. In essence, initiation is about meeting the *more of you* and choosing to step into her.

For example, think about the indigenous rite of passage into manhood. Often between the ages of 16-18 a young man is sent out into the wilderness to go on a vision quest.

For several days he must stay in the wild alone, hunting and gathering his own food and water, finding shelter, and confronting the elements. If he returns to his tribe alive at the end of the allotted time, he is officially recognized as a man. No longer a boy, he has passed the test of his first *initiation*.

For me, personally, writing this book was its own spiritual initiation. I faced many personal thresholds and obstacles throughout the writing and editorial process. There were moments of profound challenge, and times when I genuinely didn't know if I'd ever finish this book. They often say, "it's darkest before dawn." Well, I'm proud to say I've faced the dark and love the woman I see in the mirror of my dawn.

As such, I've decided to include the next two personal stories to demonstrate my own initiatory process so that you'll feel less alone when you hit yours.

The important thing to remember is this: initiations are a sign that we have asked life for *more*, and have decided to expand. When we decide to expand, life will mirror back to us all the ways in which we are still playing small. These initiations can be painful, but if we choose to face them head-on, we accelerate our path to expansion. It's like choosing to slay a dragon so we can get to a pot of gold. And sister, there is so much gold waiting for you.

The Stories We Carry: The Initiation of Truth

As my editor was completing the final revisions for this book I was initiated into a real-time confrontation of truth. Given the timing of this event, I felt strongly that it was meant to be included in the book.

One day, as I was mid-revision, reading over one of my editor's emails, I was stopped in my tracks by an interaction with my aunt. This interaction is a perfect example of what it means to **wake up in the South**, where myth often holds more weight than fact, and where stories still shape identities, even when they aren't true.

I was talking with my aunt, while looking over edits, and casually mentioned something I had forgotten I never told her: **we're not Native American.** At least, *I'm not*. My DNA test recently came back with 0 percent. My mother's did too. My grandmother, her mother, also tested with no Indigenous ancestry. So, by basic logic, if no juicy affairs happened that our immediate family would show, my aunt may be related to me and not be either.

In fact, we are actually of British descent, with some Irish and Welsh roots, tracing back to a small island called Jersey. Think more Catherine Zeta-Jones or Bella Hadid than Pocahontas or Tomochichi. Not nearly as romanticized, but far more accurate.

My aunt wasn't having it though. She was quick to repeat the story she'd been told. As if to reinforce it, she repeated the same story we had all heard growing up: her great-grandmother married a Cherokee chief. She said it with conviction. No curiosity. No hesitation. No questions.

That's when I recognized what was happening. Being *awake* to the situation.

I unintentionally had just shaken her identity. Her totalitarian ego showed up to protect her. Her psychological mechanism that exists to protect the identity she's built. When something challenges that identity, especially something as deeply ingrained as ancestral pride, the ego steps in to defend it at all costs. Repeating the belief out loud is not just stubbornness. It's the unconscious mind's way of anchoring the story, of trying to hold it in place before it slips away. It is reinforcement through ritual.

Now sure, could it be possible that my grandfather was not really my mom's biological father, and he never knew that? Could my aunt, my mother's sister, actually carry a different bloodline that makes her version of the story true? Of course that's possible. I'm not blind to the variables. My mind wasn't closed to the possibility that something complicated or unspoken may have happened in the family tree. What struck me wasn't the mystery of the missing link. It was how locked her mind was to even considering it as a truth. Her mind was closed to the fact that the story we've been told doesn't apply to me and therefore, may not apply to her either. The story was simply true to her. Not up for discussion. Not open to question. Just the way it was and always had been.

This shows how we have listened to stories passed down for generations and accepted their versions of reality as truth, the only truth. There's a possibility my grandfather believed the story he was told by the person before him and wasn't lying. Right? It doesn't make us a liar to repeat something that we learned as a truth. But it also doesn't make the lie real. It isn't a lie if you believe it. But it also isn't the truth because you believe it either. The goal in this awareness is to show belief systems at play, but also to show you that there is a chance we can be wrong more often than we'd like to admit.

Being wrong is the only way I am sure to learn anything. I live by it. I used to be obsessed with sharing what I know. Now I'm obsessed with figuring out what I don't know.

I get it. Letting go of a belief that's been passed down for generations feels like betrayal. Especially in the South, where so much of who we are is tied to where we come from or where we think we come from. It's not about fault. It's about awareness.

Maybe there was a secret love affair in our lineage. Maybe a child was passed off as someone else's. We weren't there. We can't know. What we can do is stop mistaking tradition for truth. Just because a story is old ,doesn't make it sacred. Just because someone we loved believed it, doesn't mean we have to carry it forward.

My driver's license still says Native American. Not because I'm trying to deceive anyone, but because I have not yet updated it. That check mark was once a source of pride. Now, it's a quiet reminder of how powerful stories can be, even when they're not ours to keep.

This is what waking up looks like. It's not always dramatic. Sometimes it's a phone call, a document, a truth you didn't ask for but can't ignore.

The DMV can wait. But the reckoning? That starts now.

At some point, we have to decide: Do we keep repeating the stories we were given or do we make space for the truth that's trying to rise?

Pain Into Power: A Final Prayer

As this book comes to a close, understand that something greater is ending alongside it. I am not only finishing a manuscript. I am closing a significant chapter of my life.

This work represents more than words on a page. It is a threshold I have crossed while bringing it to completion. The timing is not accidental. This month I faced a deeply personal, life-altering situation. The details of it are irrelevant, but make no mistake, it was a true initiation. The parallel between creation and transformation became undeniable. Completing this book during a season of personal unraveling and rebirth feels like the most honest metaphor I can offer. The breakdown and the breakthrough occurred simultaneously. One demanded surrender, while the other required perseverance. This is the sacred rhythm of yin and yang. Feminine yielding and masculine resilience. Both energies held space for me. Both led me back to myself. I now stand here, fully present and raw.

Perspective shapes everything. The way I choose to interpret this season grants me strength. That choice alone is a form of power.

Outside, the Southern summer presses in with intense heat and humidity. In this part of the world, we say, *"It ain't the heat that'll get cha, it's the humidity."* That statement, like most Southern idioms, holds a silly but true wisdom. Heaviness rarely comes from what is obvious.

While the sun scorches the world beyond my walls, I sit wrapped in a thermal jacket, joggers, and socks. My body is cold. My spirit is stirring. That is how I recognize change approaching. The nervous system always whispers before the mind understands and I now know how to welcome and acknowledge it. I am in the process of transmuting a painful life experience into something greater. This is not simply survival. I am using it as fuel to step fully into my next level.

True alchemy is not about turning metal into gold. It is about turning pain into power, confusion into clarity, endings into openings. Alchemy is the sacred process of choosing to transform rather than collapse. It is the ability to hold the fire of your own becoming without running from the heat. Every heartbreak, every betrayal, every ending, or unraveling in my life has asked me to transmute suffering into strength. That is the real gold. That is the kind of wealth you carry within you forever.

I could be sitting here right now, playing the victim, letting my heart ache over everything surrounding me. No one in my small circle would blame me for that, but they also know me well. That isn't my style. Instead, I am choosing to finish this book. I am not ignoring the pain, I am just using it. I am not suppressing it, I am welcoming it. That is the kind of choice I am talking about when I say life is a series of choices. This is inspired action, my love. The decision to create, to rise, to move forward even when it hurts.

Pain has accompanied me throughout my journey. I used to clutch and drag it behind me, but now I carry it in front of me softly. This book waited silently in my digital archives for over two years. I told myself I needed time to figure out how to complete it, but what I truly needed was truth. Perhaps they go hand in hand. This new truth arrived in unexpected form and pulled me back to this page. It completed this work.

Closing Prayer

May these words not act as a solution, but as a mirror. May they meet you where your soul most needs to be seen. May you feel deeply reminded of your softness, your power, and your sacred ability to begin again.

I pray that you return to these pages when your spirit calls for them. With time, we all evolve. What speaks softly now may speak thunder later. Let every line become a reflection of the person you are becoming.

Divine manifestation is not magic. It is presence. May you become ever more aware of your thoughts, your choices, and your energy. May you remember that your life unfolds through a series of aligned decisions. One conscious choice can shift your entire reality.

I give deep thanks for every version of myself that carried me here. The ones who weathered storms I now bless and release. May you, too, honor the version of you who chose not to give up. You do not need to become someone new. You only need to remember the part of you who still believes. She has not left. She has simply been waiting for you to come home.

Energy is sacred. I pray that you no longer pour it into hands that cannot hold it. May you stop bending yourself into shapes that please others while breaking yourself in the process. Love does not require shrinking. Alignment requires wholeness.

Let this truth anchor in your spirit. The moment you feel the urge to explain yourself to someone who is not willing to hear you, pause. Return to center. Do not meet them at the level of their resistance. That is not love. That is self-abandonment. May you always choose clarity over compromise.

People show up when they want to. If they wanted to, they would. May you never again internalize someone else's absence as a reflection of your worth.

You were never sent here to be someone's redemption. I pray you release the burden of healing those who refuse to heal themselves. Their wounds are not your assignment. Their chaos is not your cross.

Your presence is magnetic. Your light is real. May you never confuse desire with deserving. May you protect your attention like the sacred gift it is.

You were never made to beg. You were never made to chase. You were never made to shrink. You deserve to be met in fullness. May you stop settling for crumbs. Let them feed the pigeons. You deserve the feast.

When you accept dishonesty, disrespect, or dismissal, you do not just hurt, you disconnect from yourself. May you have the courage to stop handing your power to those who cannot be trusted to hold it.

So I ask you now, and may you ask yourself with unwavering truth:

How much do you mean to you?

Until that answer becomes unshakable, you will continue giving sacred pieces of yourself away. But you were not born for that. You were born to rise. You were born to expand. You were born to walk in truth and to be the embodiment of it.

May you protect your energy like your life depends on it. Because it does.

May the world within you shift. And may the world around you rise to meet it.

God is love

Amen.

I am choosing to move forward. Not because it is easy, but because remaining small is no longer an option. I am here to disrupt, to heal, to rebuild, and to live awake.

Winston Churchill once said, "Now this is not the end. It is not even the beginning of the end. But it is, perhaps, the end of the beginning."

This is the end of the book.
BUT the beginning of everything else.

XO- Pretty

Glossary

Abundance - A plentiful or overflowing quantity of something. In a spiritual context, it refers to a mindset and experience of having more than enough.

Affirmation - A positive statement repeated to oneself to reinforce a desired belief or reality.

Alchemy - An ancient practice involving the transformation of materials, which symbolically represents the process of spiritual transformation.

Alignment - The state of being in harmony, agreement, or arrangement with a desired frequency, energy, or goal.

Astrology - The study of movements and relative positions of celestial objects as a means for divining information about human affairs and life on earth.

Attunement - The process of aligning or bringing into harmony with a particular energy, frequency, or vibration.

Aura - The distinctive atmosphere or energy field surrounding a person or object.

Authenticity - The quality of being genuine, true, and aligned with one's core values and essence.

Awareness - The state of being conscious and having knowledge or perception of a situation or fact.

Being - The state or essential nature of existing or reality as opposed to appearance or illusion.

Chakra - Any of the seven principal energy centers in the body according to Hindu tradition.

Clairvoyance - The supposed ability to perceive things that are not present to the senses, especially through extrasensory perception.

Cognitive Biases - These are systematic patterns of deviation from rationality in judgment and decision-making. These biases often stem from the brain's attempt to simplify information processing, leading to errors in thinking, perception, and memory.

Cognitive Science - The scientific study of the mind and its processes, including how thoughts, beliefs, and emotions influence our perception and behavior. Manifestation practices draw on insights from cognitive science to understand the connection between thoughts and reality.

GLOSSARY

Collective Manifestation - The belief that a group's focused intention and energy can influence reality for the greater good.

Collective Unconscious - A concept in analytical psychology, referring to the shared unconscious beliefs and experiences of all human beings.

Consciousness - The state of being aware of one's surroundings, thoughts, and sensations.

Contrive - To contrive is to deliberately create or bring about something through skillful or clever planning. It often implies the use of ingenuity to achieve a specific outcome, sometimes in a way that seems artificial or forced.

Co-creation - The act of creating or manifesting something in collaboration with the universe or a higher power.

Divine - Of or relating to God or a deity, something sacred or holy.

Energy - The fundamental force or power allowing manifestation and transformation to occur in the universe.

Epigenetics- The study of how behaviors and environmental factors can cause changes that affect how genes work, without altering the underlying DNA sequence.

Feminine - Qualities traditionally associated with female energy such as intuition, creativity, and fluidity.

Feminine Energy (in Astrology) - Represents qualities like intuition, receptivity, nurturing, and creativity. Balancing these energies with masculine energy is believed to be beneficial for manifestation.

Flow - The state of being fully immersed and energized in an activity, experiencing a feeling of effortless concentration.

Goal Setting - The process of defining specific, measurable, achievable, relevant, and time-bound (SMART) objectives that you want to achieve. Clear goals provide direction and focus for your manifestation efforts.

Gratitude - An appreciation for what you already have in life. Practicing gratitude fosters a positive mindset and can enhance the manifestation process.

Higher Self - An idealized representation of one's greatest, most wise, and spiritually evolved inner being.

Imagination - The ability to form mental images, ideas, and concepts not present to the senses.

Intention - The conscious act of directing one's thoughts and energy towards a desired outcome or manifestation.

Integration - The process of combining or unifying different concepts, practices or experiences into a cohesive whole.

Intuition - The ability to understand or know something instinctively, without conscious reasoning.

Inspired Action - Taking action aligned with your goals and fueled by a sense of purpose and enthusiasm. Inspired action is a crucial component of successful manifestation.

Law of Attraction - The principle that likes attracts like, and that positive or negative thoughts bring about positive or negative experiences.

Limiting Beliefs - Negative thoughts or assumptions that hold you back from achieving your goals. Identifying and transforming limiting beliefs is essential for successful manifestation.

Linguistics - The scientific study of language and its structure. This field explores the rules and principles governing the use of language, including phonetics, syntax, semantics, and pragmatics, among other aspects.

Masculine Energy (in Astrology) - Represents qualities like action, assertiveness, logic, and leadership. Balancing these energies with feminine energy is believed to be beneficial for manifestation.

Manifestation - The process of bringing something into physical existence through focused intention and energy.

Materialism - A tendency to be more concerned with material possessions than spiritual or intellectual pursuits.

Meditation - A practice of concentrated focus to calm the mind and find inner peace.

Metaphysical - Relating to the transcendent or supernatural as opposed to the physical world.

Mindfulness - The practice of purposely focusing one's attention on the present moment in a non-judgmental way.

Multidimensional - Having multiple dimensions, layers, or aspects beyond the physical world.

Mysticism - Belief that union with or absorption into the Deity or divine can be attained through contemplation and self-surrender.

Nadi - A channel or pathway through which energy flows in the body.

Neuroplasticity - The ability of the brain to form new neural connections and pathways based on experience.

Paradigm - A model or worldview underlying the theories and methodology of a subject.

Perception - The way you interpret and give meaning to your experiences based on your prior conditioning.

Positivity - The practice of focusing one's thoughts and outlook on the optimistic and constructive aspects of a situation.

Presence - The state of being consciously aware and focused in the present moment.

Quantum Field - A concept of quantum theory describing the fundamental field from which all particles originate as quantized vibrations.

Reality - The world or state of things as they exist, as opposed to an idealistic or notional idea of them.

Reiki - A Japanese healing technique based on the principle of channeling universal life force energy.

Resistance - Opposition, refusal to accept or behave in a particular way.

Ritual - A ceremonial or spiritual act performed customarily.

Serenity - A state of being calm, peaceful, and untroubled.

Soul - The spiritual or immaterial part of a human being, regarded as immortal.

Subconscious - The part of the mind operating automatically outside of conscious

awareness, storing deeply rooted beliefs.

Synapse - The junction between two nerve cells, where electrical or chemical signals are transmitted from one neuron to another. It plays a crucial role in neural communication and information processing in the brain and nervous system.

Synchronicity - The coincidental occurrence of events that seem related but are not causally connected.

Transcendence - The act of rising above or going beyond ordinary limits.

Transformation - A thorough or dramatic change in form, appearance, or character.

Unconscious - The part of the mind operating automatically outside of conscious awareness, storing deeply rooted beliefs.

Universe - The totality of all existing things, including the cosmos and all realities.

Vibe/Vibration - The energy frequency or oscillating pattern something naturally resonates at.

Visualization - The practice of forming mental images or pictures to support the manifestation process.

Vortex - A spiraling flow of energy, often associated with powerful manifestation points.

Well-Being - A state of feeling healthy, happy, and prosperous in all aspects of life.

Wishful Thinking - Indulging fanciful thoughts that are unlikely to become reality due to a lack of practical action.

Wisdom - The ability to think and act using knowledge, experience, understanding and good judgment.

Woo-Woo - A lighthearted slang term for concepts considered unconventional or metaphysical.

Yin-Yang - The concept of opposing but complementary energies or forces in the universe.

Yoga - Is both a practice and a philosophy. At its core, it is the union of body, mind, and spirit. The word itself comes from Sanskrit root yuj, meaning "to yoke" or "to unite".

www.ingramcontent.com/pod-product-compliance
Lightning Source LLC
LaVergne TN
LVHW051728080426
835511LV00018B/2933